PRAISE FOR *WHY I DIDN'T REBEL*

"*Why I Didn't Rebel* is one of those treasures: a delightful *and* informative read. You laugh while you learn. Rebecca presents helpful principles without chaining us to rules and she offers many fine, real-life examples of how these principles have proven true. Well-researched, well thought-out, and well-written, *Why I Didn't Rebel* is a great book to give to young parents and for small groups to study together."

—Gary Thomas, author of *Sacred Marriage* and *Sacred Parenting*

"It's often said that '*we learn by experience.*' The truth is that we learn by experience only when we have reflected on it and done the work of articulating it. And that is at the heart of *Why I Didn't Rebel*. Drawing on her own life and dozens of her peers, Rebecca offers insights of great value for parents, most especially for parents preparing for the teen years. Read this book. Do your own reflecting on it. You will indeed learn. And both you and your children will be much the better for it!"

—Neil and Sharon Josephson, codirectors of Family Life Canada

"As a mother of four young children, I was immediately drawn to Rebecca Gregoire Lindenbach's *Why I Didn't Rebel*. Like Rebecca, I never walked through a period of rebellion—and neither did my siblings. But I've never been able to put my finger on what it was that my parents did that others couldn't mimic. Rebecca's book helped me do just that. *Why I Didn't Rebel* is a must-read for every Christian parent."

—Erin Odom, author of *More Tha*
creator of thehumbledhomemak

"If you, like me, ever feel disconnected from your child's generation or wonder if your parenting is really making a lasting difference, read Rebecca Lindenbach's book *Why I Didn't Rebel*. With humor and candid transparency, she and other young adults reveal what their parents did right and what mattered most. It's like secretly reading your child's social media posts. But this time, you have permission, so don't miss out!"

—Ron L. Deal, speaker, therapist, and author of
The Smart Stepfamily and *The Smart Stepmom*

Why
I didn't
rebel

Why I didn't rebel

A TWENTY-TWO-YEAR-OLD

EXPLAINS WHY SHE STAYED ON THE STRAIGHT
AND NARROW—*AND HOW YOUR KIDS CAN TOO*

REBECCA GREGOIRE LINDENBACH

NELSON
BOOKS

An Imprint of Thomas Nelson

Published in Nashville, Tennessee, by Nelson Books, an imprint of Thomas Nelson. Nelson Books and Thomas Nelson are registered trademarks of HarperCollins Christian Publishing, Inc.

Published in association with MacGregor Literary, www.macgregorliterary.com.

Thomas Nelson titles may be purchased in bulk for educational, business, fund-raising, or sales promotional use. For information, please e-mail SpecialMarkets@ThomasNelson.com.

ISBN 978-0-7180-9017-3 (eBook)

Library of Congress Cataloging-in-Publication Data

ISBN 978-0-7180-9000-5
Names: Lindenbach, Rebecca Gregoire, 1995- author.
Title: Why I didn't rebel : a twenty-two-year-old explains why she stayed on the straight and narrow--and how your kids can too / Rebecca Gregoire Lindenbach.
Description: Nashville : Thomas Nelson, 2017. | Includes bibliographical references.
Identifiers: LCCN 2017006564 | ISBN 9780718090005
Subjects: LCSH: Parenting--Religious aspects--Christianity. | Child rearing--Religious aspects--Christianity. | Children--Religious life. | Obedience. | Obedience--Religious aspects--Christianity.
Classification: LCC BV4529 .L553 2017 | DDC 248.8/45--dc23 LC record available at https://lccn.loc.gov/2017006564

Printed in the United States of America

17 18 19 20 21   LSC   10 9 8 7 6 5 4 3 2 1

To Mom and Dad:
Thank you for being the kind of
parents I hope to become someday.

CONTENTS

INTRODUCTION

HOW THIS BOOK ALL STARTED

I never intended to write a book. Even though I finished twelve journals between the ages of ten and fourteen, I never saw myself actually writing for a *real* audience.

My first blog was called *Becca the Great*. I was ten at the time and a little overconfident, but I now find it ironic considering that a decade later I am writing a book about how my parents did a good job raising me. (I swear I'm not a narcissist.) My mother is an author and speaker, so I've always been a part of the writing world, though I never particularly wanted to join it myself. I'm a psychology student, though, so I sometimes wonder if my dismissal of writing as a career is more about my trying to avoid becoming a carbon copy of my mom than an actual lack of desire.

Either way, I have obviously failed in my original plan, because here I am—the author of a book.

One day a couple of years ago, my mom was frustrated with her blog readers and decided to make it my problem. She called me and complained that whenever she wrote about parenting, there would follow a running thread of comments that all said, "Teenagers just go off the rails. It's inevitable, and you can't blame me for my kids' mistakes."

Now, while both my mother and I completely agree that the parent should not be blamed, we also don't think that all kids are guaranteed to rebel in their teenage years. My mom, however, had been trying for years without success to convince her readers there are things you can do to help keep your children from rebelling. She had been thinking about how to address the issue in a fresh way when she started wondering if people would listen more if it came from a different source—if it came from a kid who truly didn't rebel. So she asked me to write her a blog post.

I said no.

But not long afterward I found myself sitting in a statistics class, bored out of my skull, trying not to let my prof catch me watching YouTube videos of corgis, when I decided that I should do something more useful with my time. A half hour later I e-mailed the blog post off to my mom to be published.

Within three weeks over a quarter of a million people had read my post on my mother's website. I couldn't go on Pinterest without seeing my face, and radio stations called me for interviews.

I had struck a nerve. People were raving about this post. Finally given a chance to talk about teenage rebellion, people ran with it. They shared stories, gave encouragement, and asked so many questions that I couldn't possibly address them all.

My mom and I talked over the phone about everything that

happened. I was ready to move on to the next thing, but she asked, "How do you feel about writing a book?"

I thought about it, and I said no.

Do you see a pattern here?

Even though I had said no, I couldn't ignore the fact that God was opening doors. I have watched a lot of my friends' parents agonize over the choices their children have made, and I have been hurt watching my friends make terrible decisions, so if my insights could help in any way, I needed to do something.

The generation gap is huge right now. Sure, there's always been a gap. But teenagers today are facing things that their parents never did. My mom got her first computer at nineteen, but she didn't even use e-mail until I was born. She got her first Facebook account at thirty-eight; I opened mine on my thirteenth birthday.

I think the reason so many people responded to my post is because parents want to hear from a kid like their own that we really can be okay, and that despite everything we see in the media, we teenagers really can make good decisions. There are so many parenting theories and resources that try to teach parents, but maybe what they really need sometimes is a bit of encouragement, not another lecture. I hope I can encourage you with this book.

1

WHAT IS REBELLION?

IT'S NOT AS STRAIGHTFORWARD AS WE THINK

I lost my first front tooth because my little sister punched me in the face. Of course, the first time I saw her I hit her on the head, so I had it coming. At the time of the tooth incident, I was five and Katie was three, and we were cuddling with Mom while she tried to read us a story. My sister has always been extremely possessive of both of my parents, so with a resounding, "Back off, buster! Go find your own mom!" she popped me in the mouth and out flew my tooth.

My childhood was full of s'mores in the summer, falling out of my chair laughing at dinnertime, and trying to convince my mother that tutus were perfectly acceptable church wear. We made a fort in the backyard out of a rotting old shed where Katie and I played for hours at a time, pretending we were part of *Little House on the Prairie*. The first song I ever learned was "Jesus Loves Me," and I didn't realize that some people didn't know God until I was five years old and one of my kindergarten friends didn't know how to say grace before lunch.

Of course, I got into some mischief too. I got in trouble more times than I can count for using Katie as my guinea pig for various experiments. Like the "Let's see if this is safe to eat or if it will make you throw up" experiment or the "If I pull away your chair at the last moment, how high will you bounce off the floor?" experiment. I don't know why she trusted me so much.

I had a happy childhood, but that doesn't mean it was perfect. Our family was marked by loss, as I had a brother who passed away before Katie was born. My parents, although wonderful, both had tempers and yelled at me too much. I've always struggled with emotion-regulation issues, starting with intense tantrums at age two and continuing into some pretty dark phases in my teenage years. I cried over boys, was betrayed by friends, and fought with my sister.

But I never rebelled.

I had my own issues, yes, and I wasn't anywhere near perfect, but at the end of the day I was the kid who honored her parents. They gave me a happy childhood that has followed me into adulthood, and one day, when I have kids, I hope I can do the same for them. My mom and dad definitely did something right.

WHAT IS REBELLION?

Before I can be your family's cheerleader to raise rebellion-resistant kids, I'm going to spend the rest of this chapter clearing up what rebellion is—and what it isn't. I can't tell you how to raise children who will do everything you want them to, who won't ever make mistakes, and who won't ever be moody or hormonal. What I do want to do is share with you the stories of parents who raised kids to run after God, because that's what I hope we're all aiming for.

Unfortunately, that's not the normal definition for a "good kid." Usually, when we talk about rebellion, we're talking about going against authority—especially parental authority—and a good kid is a kid who always does exactly what he or she is told and never makes a fuss. I don't think I've ever known a kid like that, but I do know many children who haven't rebelled. So let's expand our definition of what rebellion *isn't*.

TEENAGE TRANSITION IS NOT REBELLION

When I was twelve my sister drew a picture of me with devil horns. That pretty much summarized our relationship then. The years when I hit puberty while my sister was still a child were especially hard. I screamed and cried, she screamed and hit, and my poor mother felt like a failure. Two years later, after Katie had gone through puberty as well, we were friends again.

Teenagers are just plain annoying. They're hormonal, they're moody, and they think they're better than you because for the first time in their lives they can logically reason through things (though they don't have the experience to show them they're actually quite naïve). Teens are going to do things that parents don't understand, whether it's wearing crazy shoes or watching stupid movies saturated with fart jokes.

Adolescence is a unique time of life when one can try out pretty much anything and not have to make any commitments. In fact, Erik Erikson, one of the most influential developmental psychologists ever, coined the term *psychosocial moratorium* to describe this phenomenon.[1] Psychosocial moratorium means that society has decided it's perfectly acceptable for teens to try things that are taboo at any other age, since they're at a crossroads where they're trying to form their identity. Dyeing their hair pink or wearing certain clothes, for instance, might not be appropriate at twenty-five or forty but is completely okay for a fifteen-year-old, socially speaking. Children need this time of transition where they go from being who their parents say they are to who they decide they are.

Often, though, when thinking of a moody teenager, it's easy for parents to just see a troublesome kid who needs more discipline. But although, yes, it is important to learn emotional self-discipline techniques, it is not rebellion to be a moody teenager. A thirteen-year-old girl going through all the horrors of PMS for the first time is not going to be docile, sweet, and selfless. She's just not. She's going to resemble something along the lines of an anaconda mixed with a tiger that has a thorn in its foot and is hunting for blood. How parents handle a child's natural transition from kid to teenager has a lot of power. Are you the kind of parent who hugs her daughter while she cries and tells her, "I know; everything is horrible when your uterus tries to eat its way out of you," or do you tell your cramping, PMS-ing daughter, "Honey, the Bible says, 'In everything give thanks,' so you really need to work on being gracious and thankful right now"? God created the female reproductive system. I'm pretty sure He has sympathy for cramps.

My poor father had it bad. He had two daughters, both of whom were emotionally volatile, going through puberty and all the social upheavals that happen along with high school at practically the same time (we're only two years apart). I will tell you: the years between my twelfth and sixteenth birthdays were dark times in the Gregoire household. My parents, however, handled us very well. I remember that whenever my teenage angst was particularly distressing for me, my dad would bring home ice cream or popcorn, and we would watch a movie together. He didn't ever have to talk to me about my teenage issues (except for when I wanted to talk, of course), but just knowing that he understood my utter anguish was comforting to me.

Being a teenager is not a sin. Going through transition is not a sin, and it is okay to allow your children to feel the intense emotions that come with adolescence. My parents allowed us the freedom to grow and develop by acknowledging how difficult those years can be, and our relationship is stronger for it.

PERSONALITY CLASHES ARE NOT REBELLION

I think we also need to expand our ideas about what being a good kid really means. When we think of a good kid, we think of one who doesn't have a problem listening to authority or who is always smiling and happy and in touch with how the people around him or her are feeling. We think of the girl who can go into any room and make five friends, who never wears heavy makeup, and who always wears a purity ring on her left hand. We think of the boy who loves to help with the kids in Sunday school, who is soft-spoken, but who is also a leader.

Often our examples of a "good girl" or a "good guy," though, are based more around personality than around character traits. But my personality is the complete opposite of your average good kid.

I'm opinionated, I despise rules, and I don't take no for an answer. I am driven, competitive, and independent—probably the opposite of what most people picture *feminine* to be. I'm pretty sure God put me on this earth for the sole purpose of stirring up trouble by pointing out where others are wrong. I may not have been the typical "perfect" feminine Christian teenager, but I can also assure you that despite my intense, contrary personality, I never rebelled.

I was the kid who did my schoolwork, who marched off to my job (even at 5:45 a.m. to a cold pool at the YMCA), and who memorized the Bible in my spare time. I'm not even kidding about the last one—my sister and I were involved in a Bible-quizzing program, and we both made it to the international level multiple years running. I have memorized all of Galatians, Ephesians, Philippians, Colossians, Hebrews, 1 and 2 Peter, 1 and 2 Corinthians, John, and most of Luke.

I never drank, never partied, and had never even kissed a

boy until I met the man I married. All this despite the fact that in high school many of my friends were heavily into the party scene, smoked pot every once in a while, and were openly having sex. I wasn't sheltered, I wasn't naturally submissive, but I always respected and honored my parents' decisions, even when many others were doing the opposite.

When I was in junior high, I attended an amazing weekly youth group. There was a great group of high school kids who were strong in their faith, and they all looked out for me and took care of me. By the time I reached high school, though, that youth group had started to shift. The kids who'd been so strong had graduated or moved away, and the leadership changed. It slowly continued to slip until one day I realized it had fallen somewhere bad. I remember walking into one of the weekend overnighters, hearing Lady Gaga blasting from the speakers in the dimly lit basement, and seeing girls dancing on the pool table in short shorts and tank tops, with the leaders watching and laughing. My church's basement had become someplace dirty, and I was heartbroken.

So, at only fifteen, I phoned my youth leader and confronted him. I had my dad sitting beside me for emotional and moral support, and I remember my hands shaking as I punched in the numbers. It rang and rang, and eventually he picked up.

I'm not quite sure what I expected, but that conversation did not go well. I told the leader that what was happening in the youth group was not at all God-honoring—the music videos with half-naked girls, the explicit songs, the language (sure, I'd heard the f-word before, but I knew it wasn't appropriate in a church basement), and especially the table dancing.

I suppose I expected him to see the truth of the matter, but that is not what happened. Instead, this man who was running the youth group told little tenth-grade me that I was judgmental and that I needed to understand what God's love really meant. The conversation ended shortly after with me in tears and my dad stroking my hair.

The next year or so was a blur of confrontation. I was not able to let this be—even though it meant telling every single leader of the church that what was happening on Friday youth nights was wrong. Even though it meant standing up to everyone I was supposed to submit to not only as a young person in general, but as a young person under church leadership.

Many people in my church supported my cause, but many didn't. I lived for two years feeling so ostracized that I started sitting with the sixth-grade kids because they were the only ones who didn't hate me. The leaders and people who had formerly been my friends called me "traitor"—among other mean names—after I began attending a different youth group. They even tried to turn my sister against me. They told her that they loved her and that they wouldn't judge her based on her family, because they knew that she wasn't judgmental or a goody two-shoes like I was. As soon as my parents learned this they were furious, and both Katie and I left the youth program at the church for good.

It took two years for the senior leadership of the church to finally realize how bad things had gotten, but at that point it was already too late. The church had lost its Christian high school youth and had gained a bad reputation. Four years later the church's youth program finally got back on its feet—and only then because the entire leadership and student body had turned over. I'm on good terms now with those I fought against, but it was a very rough road for a long time.

Many people in the church thought I was overstepping my bounds. I was causing trouble, stirring up mischief, making mountains out of molehills. Since I was questioning leadership instead of trusting them, I wasn't respecting authority and was being impertinent. I was just a little girl. What did I know, anyway? I wasn't the good kid in that situation; my church's entire youth ministry was against me because in that moment, with that phone call, I was the one who was rebelling.

QUESTIONING AUTHORITY IS NOT AUTOMATICALLY REBELLION

I have to ask myself, though, was it really rebellion? When we think of the kid who doesn't rebel, we tend to think of someone who doesn't make waves. He's the kid who is happy all the time, has a few good friends, and doesn't hang out with the bad kids. She picks up her laundry off the floor and helps with dishes after dinner. He goes to church and plays piano for worship. She doesn't decide to tell the pastors that they are doing something wrong, and she definitely doesn't create conflict within church leadership.

But is that accurate? In my situation I know I did the right thing. Today the church youth group is once again a safe place in which Christian kids can worship God and invite their friends to encounter the real Jesus. But back then it was not. I saw God's house being misused and disrespected, and I addressed it. The cost was discomfort and conflict, but I stood up for what was right.

So is a kid who doesn't rebel really someone who doesn't rock the boat? No—a good kid is one who listens to God's voice and does what he or she is called to do.

Sometimes following God's plan means shaking things up. When we think a good kid is synonymous with a placid kid, we're limiting the ways God can work through that child. Some people are primarily meant to be peacekeepers. Others, though, are meant to be warriors, and it's important to be able to see the difference between making waves and making trouble.

What it boils down to is this: true rebellion is not rebelling against parents or against other earthly authority—it's rebelling against God. When I stood up against my church, I rebelled against my church leadership, and to be honest, even my dad wasn't completely on board at the beginning. (Once he saw for himself what was happening and how my leader was treating me, though, trust me—he got on board.) However, I was not rebelling against God. I was making everyone else's life pretty difficult, but it wasn't rebellion, because I was trying to honor God.

In fact, I think that sometimes going against your parents is the right thing to do and is not an act of rebellion either. What happens if following God's call means you must forsake your parents?

In our neighborhood there was only one other homeschooling family, but unlike ours, that one had a whole pile of kids. Also unlike us, they didn't continue the girls' education past eighth grade, because that's when they started training their daughters to become wives and mothers, concentrating on sewing, canning, and housekeeping skills. They completely sheltered their children. One time all the teen homeschoolers were at a Bible study together, and those girls weren't allowed to stay for the video sermon we had brought. "You never know what will be on a video," they were told. (That particular video series was Francis Chan talking about love.) Their parents confined them to their own very narrow definition of *housewives*.

These girls, in my opinion, should have rebelled against their parents. They should have said that they wanted an education, that they could do more than just cook and clean for the rest of their lives. Now, being a housewife can be a wonderful and fulfilling life goal—if God has called you to be a full-time mom and wife. But what if God has called one of these girls to be a surgeon who does missions in Nepal? Or what if one of these girls never gets married? The way their parents raised them has limited the ways they can serve God or even provide for themselves if necessary.

I grew up with a friend named Samuel whose family was extremely involved in a local church. This church was their family's "thing"; it was what they did—and what they had been doing for generations. The family environment, though, was neither warm nor caring. Samuel frequently clashed with his parents. He didn't feel understood, and the church they attended wasn't giving him what he needed to grow spiritually, which he longed for. When he became an adult, he told his parents that he was switching churches. They did not take it well. They even excluded him from many family functions. For Samuel, leaving the church meant he was no longer welcome in his own family. But was it rebellion to follow God's call for his life instead of his parents'? I don't think so.

The idea that children should never go against their parents is not even biblical. Look at Jonathan and Saul—in 1 Samuel 19 Jonathan went directly against Saul's clear orders to kill David. He did so because he was David's friend. He followed what he knew was right over what was asked of him.

More important, look at Jesus' words in Luke 14:26: "If anyone comes to me and does not hate father and mother, wife and children, brothers and sisters—yes, even their own life—such a person cannot be my disciple." That means if you follow Jesus, you must be willing to forsake your own family. Sometimes God's calling for us as children means that we go against our parents. The trick is in knowing when that is our calling.

This book, then, isn't about showing how parents raised kids who never rebelled against them. Instead, it's showing how parents raised kids who didn't rebel against God.

MAKING A MISTAKE IS NOT REBELLION

Nothing in this book is going to tell you how to raise a perfect kid, because the scenario of raising the perfect kid doesn't exist. But just because your kid isn't perfect doesn't mean he is automatically rebellious. Everyone has sinned, and all of us naturally fight against God. In fact, technically, all of us have rebelled. Jesus came down and has reconciled us to Himself, but that doesn't mean we don't still sin. Hear me on this: making a mistake is not the same thing as actively living a sinful life. There is a big difference between the kid who sneaks out every Friday night to party while pretending everything is perfect on Sunday and the girl who gets drunk once and comes home crying and apologizing to her parents. The second mistake is neither good nor okay. Nor should it be ignored. But while parents need to expect greatness from their children, there is a difference between expecting greatness and demanding perfection.

All hope is not lost when your child makes a mistake . . . or two or even three. Look at King David—he committed adultery and then murdered the woman's husband. And yet he was a man after God's own heart (1 Sam. 13:14; Acts 13:22). Of course, it wasn't that God didn't care about David's sin, but He saw true repentance and the anguish David was going through because of his sin. And because of that repentance, God forgave him.

I definitely hope your child doesn't commit adultery and then murder someone, but the point remains: mistakes do not mean your child is tainted or a bad kid; it just means she is human. If she truly seeks out God in the midst of her brokenness, that is the sign of a good child, not a rebellious one.

I don't want you to just take my word for it regarding rebellion. I'm only twenty-two, and I'm only one girl from one family. My story doesn't begin to cover the topic of teenage rebellion. So I've brought in some others to help unravel what parents can do to help their children not rebel.

THE PEOPLE IN THE BOOK

This book is not just an account of how my parents raised me to be a good kid. I have also gathered stories from friends, friends of friends, and people I've met through my blog. I made sure all the people mentioned here are between the ages of eighteen and twenty-five, so at least they were still teenagers while Facebook and other social media platforms were taking off. (Social media has so changed the teenage experience that, to be relevant, I could only include people who had lived through that as teens themselves.) I've interviewed people from a range of backgrounds—they don't all come from your typical perfect nuclear Christian family. I've interviewed twenty-five young adults from a wide variety of educational, socioeconomic, and family backgrounds to make sure you will have at least one story you can see as *your* story.

After talking to many of my friends and then others who were referred to me by people who heard about my book, I found eight different points that successful families shared. Essentially, though, they all boil down to this: successful parents aren't perfect; rather, they're authentic, and they expect the same from their children. So much parenting advice—especially in the Christian community—is about controlling your child's behavior, starting at a young age. We're told, "Spare the rod, spoil the child," and that rigid rules about dating and courtship are the only way your child will remain pure. But what I've found is that parents who try to bring out the best in their children, rather than just suppress the worst, end up with much better relationships—and, ironically, far less need for discipline.

Since it's based primarily on long interviews with people I chose, this book is not a scientific study—although as a psychology student I can't help but bring in various studies to show that my friends' and my successes are actually quite typical. It's also not a checklist for how to create the perfect kid. Instead, I want to help us rethink what it means to have a good relationship with our kids.

Unfortunately, there can never be any guarantee your kid will not rebel. Look at the prodigal son: in Jesus' parable the father represented God, and even he had a boy who went off the rails. God's children turn away from Him all the time, and He is the ultimate Father.

Just because there isn't a guarantee, though, does not mean it's hopeless and you should give up. Let's think about rebellion as being like lung cancer. Anyone can get lung cancer, but if you're afraid of getting it, you don't smoke. It's not a guarantee by any stretch of the imagination—everyone knows of that one thirty-five-year-old marathon-running vegan woman with lung cancer despite all odds. But just because one thirty-five-year-old woman can get lung cancer doesn't mean you should just give up trying to avoid things that cause cancer and start smoking. That would be foolish.

It's the same with the things I've put in this book—none of these will ever be able to guarantee your child will do what is right, but they help make it more likely. These are behaviors and tools that have worked for other families, and I hope that by taking them into consideration, you and your children may also be able to share a close and trusting bond. That's what my family did, and that bond is one of the things I'm most grateful for in this life. I hope and pray more parents and kids can experience it together.

2

RULES VERSUS REASONS

WHEN "BECAUSE I SAID SO" DOESN'T CUT IT

Skating every Friday with our local homeschooling group was the highlight of the week for my sister and me. She'd don her crimson-and-orange skating outfit and twirl and jump while I'd stick padding everywhere I could and join the hockey game with the boys. One day, as I was skating past the moms, I heard one mother mutter, "No daughter of mine would ever be seen in jeans. Nice girls don't wear denim."

This sentiment was frequently heard from that particular mother, and despite always dressing in what I felt was an appropriate manner, I caught her shaking her head at what I was wearing way too many times to count. Even though I knew I wasn't doing anything wrong, I felt such shame at her words that day. Despite the fact that in my eyes tears are a weakness, I fled to the bathroom and cried for a few minutes before going out on the ice.

This family epitomized a rules-based family, with tons of strict rules, such as the one about denim. The girls weren't allowed to be alone in a room with any boy, even if they were just friends and their dad was in the next room. They weren't allowed to watch any videos, even Christian ones, in case there was something objectionable in it. And the only music they were allowed to listen to was the chanting of Scripture, like monks in the sixteenth century. It was pretty intense.

My family was pretty much the opposite. I can't remember any specific rules at all—there weren't any about what movies we could watch or what music we could listen to, and although there was a "No closed doors" policy with guys, it was more of an understanding than a set-in-stone rule. My parents gave us guidelines and reasons for why we should or should not do something. Instead of having a "No fuzzy boas upstairs in the living room" rule, we were told, "Daddy is allergic to your fluffy dress-up clothes, so we keep them downstairs so Daddy can breathe." Since we wanted Daddy to be able to breathe, we kept our fluffy dress-up clothes downstairs and made sure our friends never brought them upstairs either. Having these reasons made sense, and I generally agreed with them.

As we got older, those guidelines became much more flexible. When I was fifteen my parents weren't too crazy about me video chatting with male friends, and that became a point of tension for us. But we discussed it. I explained that I wouldn't video chat with boys they didn't know, and I would never add anyone I met online. Since most of my good friends lived in different cities, it didn't make any sense for me not to be able to talk to them. They agreed, and the rule changed.

At the same time, many of the rules I wanted to change, didn't. There was one time I tried to convince my dad that my sister should have to do more chores than I did because she was more annoying. That one backfired. But we always had that conversation, and it was always clear why my parents didn't change their minds. Usually I agreed.

When I started to write a chapter on rules, I found it very difficult, considering I didn't feel as though I'd ever had any. But there must be a difference between families with a rule for everything, families with no rules at all, and families with reasons instead of rules. So what is the perfect balance? Let's look at the stories of Megan and Nathan to try to figure this out.

NO RULES: THE PROBLEM OF TOO MUCH FREEDOM TOO SOON

When I first met Megan in the tenth grade, she was on fire for God. She told me at the time, though, that it was a relatively new development. In junior high Megan had been a bit of a wild child, so when I interviewed her for the book, I was interested in finding out why she had been so seduced by the wild side.

"My family didn't have a lot of rules," Megan explained, "and the ones we had were never really enforced. I was taught how to negotiate to get what I want and not to obey my parents or respect them. If I wanted something, I always got it either by bargaining with my parents or by just doing whatever it was anyway, since I knew they wouldn't really do anything to stop me."

One of the spoken rules in Megan's house was that if she was going to open a social media account, her parents needed to have her password. However, though her parents said they wanted her passwords, they never actually asked for them. Megan simply opened a Facebook account without her parents following through on their rule. This was extremely common in Megan's house—her parents would say one thing but then never follow through.

To try to regain control, Megan's mom would yell at her and her dad would say he was disappointed, and these huge fights became increasingly common when the teenage years hit. "When I did something wrong," Megan said, "I was just chastised and then we moved on. There were no real consequences, and generally I felt that what I wanted to do was worth the screaming match, so I had no reason to stop."

Every now and then, though, her parents saw there was something that needed to be addressed and that the screaming wasn't working. So they tried to lay down the law with some Scripture. "My parents were very strong Christians," Megan told me, "so the rare times when they wanted a rule to stick, they always framed it with the Bible. It was 'Don't hit your sister because the Bible says so.' But that didn't matter to me because, frankly, I didn't care what the Bible said. I didn't have much of a reason to since I didn't believe it myself, so just saying, 'God says not to' wasn't good enough. But that was the only reason they ever gave for any of the rules."

At age twelve Megan started to rebel against what her parents said God wanted for her. She didn't listen to her parents, and she got involved in casual—but very physical—dating. "Even though I didn't ever get drunk or do drugs or have sex," Megan said adamantly, "I was definitely not a good kid."

Luckily, this phase did end. When I first met her, she had just recently encountered the real Jesus, although she was still dealing with a lot of the ramifications of what happened, both in her relationship with her parents and her relationships with guys. When I asked her what she thought the major issue was that made her rebel, she told me this: "I was given too much freedom way too early. Kids need structure, and I was making my own decisions when I was eight years old. That's too much freedom for someone that young."

HAVING TOO MANY RULES: THE PROBLEM OF NOT HAVING ENOUGH FREEDOM

If having no rules can backfire, is the answer to multiply the rules instead? Let's look at a family who had lots of rules and see if they fared any better.

Nathan's family moved the year Nathan was going into his senior year of high school because his mom got a better job in a different city. The move was hard on Nathan; although he understood completely why they had to move, he had a difficult time accepting it. He had great friends back in his hometown, but the new town had a pretty wild teen culture. His new social circle lived to party and drink. Slowly, Nathan started getting more and more steeped in his new surroundings until he was one of the party kids himself.

It wasn't just the partying that was an issue, though—it was more that he did not have a good relationship with his mom. He talked back; he and his mom frequently yelled at each other. He just didn't have much respect for her.

Nathan's mom had grown up in an extremely conservative, fundamentalist Christian family. Her parents controlled their children, and what the parents said was law. When she had her own household, she never backed down from a decision because, in her mind, that showed weakness. She made all the rules, but she wouldn't explain why any of the rules were in place. Those rules were never open for discussion either, which was a major source of frustration for Nathan, because there seemed to be no rationale for them.

Nathan told me, "There was never any explanation given for the rules because there simply wasn't a coherent one. I'd be allowed to bike alone forty-five minutes into town at night, but I wouldn't be allowed to go to a friend's house in the middle of the day down the block if his parents weren't home. The rules didn't make any sense—they were just built on what Mom was feeling in that moment." Nathan shrugged. "By the time I was in grade twelve, I figured I was old enough to move out in a matter of months, so I just started following the rules that made sense to me and ignoring the ones that didn't."

Nathan's mom was very insecure about maintaining her authority over the home, and because of that she often lost control of her temper. "My mom didn't fight fair," Nathan explained. "She'd bring up things that happened in the past just so she could make me feel bad about what I was doing instead of dealing with the problem at hand."

Nathan, who is now twenty-two and looking back with lots of hindsight, sighed. "I know a lot of that is because of her past. She grew up in a really controlling environment, so I think that's all she ever knew."

But even though Nathan now understands the dynamic, he still found it frustrating. Nathan's mom saw apologizing as a sign of weakness. So even if she yelled and said hurtful things in anger, she would not apologize for what she said, which deeply affected Nathan's relationship with her. Nathan explained, "It was a constant power struggle, so I never apologized either—I couldn't give her that power, since I was afraid she'd lord it over me later."

What is so interesting about Nathan's experience is that everything negative he saw his mom doing, his dad did the opposite. His dad was much more logical in his approach to parenting, and he was willing to sit and discuss rules with his two boys, as well as explain where their mom was coming from when she was angry. Often he disagreed with their mother and they would work together to find a compromise.

"Mom treated us like little boys," Nathan explained, "but Dad always saw us as young men. When he had to talk to us about something we did wrong, he always did it with respect. We would talk as equals. When Mom disciplined us, though, we felt patronized."

Nathan also found that there wasn't that struggle for

control with his dad. If his dad ever lost his temper, he would go to Nathan when he had cooled off and apologize. "There was one fight," Nathan recalled, "when I hadn't done my chores before leaving to go to a friend's house. Dad lost his temper and screamed at me, Mom was yelling, and it was just a mess. I was furious. Later, though, Dad came upstairs and found me in my room and said, 'I'm sorry I lost my temper. That wasn't right of me, and it wasn't fair to you. Can you please forgive me for yelling at you like that?' I really respected him for that, and it made me want to listen to him more. I didn't feel the same way with Mom. With her, it was all about control."

Nathan and his mom have never had a very close relationship, although they are both very involved in each other's lives and Nathan does truly love her. "I know that most of how my mom parented was because of what she went through as a kid," Nathan said. "But that didn't mean it didn't bother me. Just because I understand why doesn't mean I was okay with it."

With his dad, however, he has a great relationship, even today, and as Nathan prepares to become a first-time father, it's his dad he goes to for advice. He sees him as a strong man that he truly respects.

Nathan's dad was not perfect. He did damage control more often than he involved himself with the day-to-day parenting Nathan's mom had taken upon herself. And Nathan probably would have had a better relationship with his mom if his parents had talked more together about what was appropriate and what wasn't, since Nathan's dad often didn't agree with his wife's parenting choices. But having one parent that Nathan could have an adult conversation with helped bring him back from those rebellious years.

Today Nathan is married, his wife is expecting their first child, and he has recently joined the union of prison guards. When I asked him what he'll do differently with his child, he told me, "I'm realizing now how difficult it must be to parent and how afraid for me my mom must have been. But even though I think she was trying to help us by having all those rules, I am going to focus more on respecting my children than controlling them. I want to make a home where my kids can grow into young men and women, where they are free to make their own choices and feel trusted by their parents."

REASONS, NOT RULES:
FINDING THE RIGHT BALANCE

Nathan believes that having rules made him more likely to rebel. But Megan knows that having no rules isn't an option either. So what's the middle ground?

Something I consistently found across my interviews with kids who didn't rebel was that none of us could really explain how we learned what was allowed. Rather, it was an ongoing conversation about right and wrong and about what was going on in that moment.

For Katie and me it meant conversations around story time or when problems arose that we disagreed about, like my wanting to video chat with my friends. But I honestly think that by the time I was thirteen, I really didn't have any rules anymore. It was about choosing right versus choosing wrong—not what we were allowed or not allowed to do.

It was tricky for a lot of us to put our fingers on just how we learned what to do or what not to do. Here's how some of the people I interviewed explained it:

- "What we did or didn't do was less of a rule and more of a reality that the family accepted. For example, we didn't have a 'Don't hit your sister' rule. It was just a reality that you don't hit each other."
- "My parents didn't really have rules, just expectations that we would be well behaved. They expected us to be good people, not to stay away from a list of behaviors. That was just assumed, because they thought highly of us."
- "I don't think we really had rules, but instead we were taught how to make good choices. For instance, when I was in high school and was going out with friends, I'd ask my parents what time they needed me home. Instead of giving me a curfew, they'd ask me, 'What time do you think you should be home tonight?' and then I'd have to make a good decision based on whether or not I had a test in the morning or if I'd be too tired to drive safely after a certain time. Honestly, I hated it at the time, but it forced me to reason through what was smart and what was a less-wise decision. Through that, I really learned how to make the right decision by myself instead of relying on my parents to do it for me."

That pretty much summed it all up—we weren't raised to simply obey rules without a thought. Instead, all of us had parents who enforced moral codes of behavior rather than lots of dos and don'ts. Instead of having rules, Katie and I were taught to live with godly morals, raised to rely on our own judgment and to seek out God's heart, and encouraged to discuss the rules and challenge them so that we learned *why* they were there. This taught us how to make good, smart decisions independently. I debated everything with my parents. If you want to really understand something, debate it with someone ten times smarter than you. It works pretty well—or at least it did for me!

Looking at the stories of Megan, Nathan, and those of us who didn't rebel, we have three scenarios: families with many rules where parents are very controlling (Nathan), families with no rules where the kids run the house (Megan), and families where the kids were taught to make good decisions (those of us in this book who didn't rebel). Perhaps not surprisingly, psychology research has found the exact same thing.

Most families fit within one of three major parenting styles: permissive, authoritarian, or authoritative. Each parenting style is marked by its amount of warmth and its amount of control. Permissive parents are very low control but very high warmth.[1] This is Megan's family's style. These parents do not assert much authority over their children since they neither enforce rules nor effectively discipline.

Authoritarian parents are on the other side of the spectrum: low warmth, high control.[2] Nathan's mom is a typical authoritarian parent: lots of rules, little give. Kids can't ask "Why not?"

in these families—it's seen as disrespectful, and questioning anything that Mom or Dad says isn't acceptable.

Authoritative parents are a healthy mix of the best of both. They are high in both control and warmth.[3] Without exception, this is where those I interviewed who didn't rebel fit in. These parents make what is expected of their children very clear but are willing to explain why they have those standards and to discuss the rules with their kids. They are also high in warmth, so although they do discipline, there is a great deal of positive interaction that heavily outweighs the negative.

When discussing the three parenting styles, though, permissive parents and authoritarian parents can often think they're authoritative. Permissive parents think they're authoritative and strict because they yell at their children, as we saw with Megan's story. My dad (a pediatrician) has many parents come into his office with children with behavior problems. Time and time again he must explain to parents that yelling is not a consequence. Yelling is a reaction—it's you getting angry. But it doesn't actually teach your child how to make better choices. It's important to look at the patterns in the family surrounding boundaries and consequences, and if yelling is your main form of discipline, odds are you're a permissive parent—especially if the kids don't really seem to care when you yell.

Authoritarian parents, too, can think they're authoritative because they really love their children and don't see themselves as low warmth. However, even if a parent has a good relationship with his or her kids and really loves them, if the relationship is marked by a power struggle and the rules are laid down as law, odds are that parent is an authoritarian parent, no matter how much the parent loves his or her kid.

The interesting part of this research is that although families with no rules and families with strict rules look so different, their children often end up in the same place: making poor decisions. In contrast, kids from authoritative families thrive. They're more likely to do well in school,[4] abstain from risk-taking behavior (such as drugs, alcohol, or sex), and have much better relationships with their parents. On the other hand, kids from authoritarian and permissive homes are much more likely to become aggressive and have other behavioral conduct problems,[5] as well as suffer from anxiety or depression.

I think that makes sense. My family was the epitome of the authoritative parenting–style family. Everything had a reason—even why we had to obey in the first place was explained. I remember when I was seven and Katie was just five, my mom was reading *Little House in the Big Woods* to us from the Little House on the Prairie series. There was a scene where Ma goes outside with Laura, thinking that the cow has gotten out. When she goes to smack the cow to usher it into the barn, though, she freezes as she recognizes that what she thought was her cow is actually a bear. She tells Laura to go back inside quickly without making a sound, and Laura obeys without question. Then Ma slowly walks away and they are all safe.

My mom used that opportunity to explain to us why it is so important that we listen when she asks us to do something. "Sometimes," Mom said, "there's something dangerous going on and I need to be sure that you two will listen to me if I ask you to do something. It's because I want you to be safe, and because I'm a grown-up, I know more about staying safe than you do." Even though they expected us to obey them, my parents did not demand that we listen without giving us a reason. Instead, they used examples like this to show us why obedience was necessary.

The major strength of the authoritative parenting style, according to the interviews I've done, is that it helped all of us learn to think for ourselves and make our own positive choices. My parents' mentality was that they were raising kids to be good people, not just kids who were well behaved. They wanted to raise us to be independent and to turn to God to figure out what's right, rather than to blindly follow their rules. In fact, they were often most proud of me when I made my own choice in a morally grey area when they hadn't told me what to do—like when I called out my youth pastor in tenth grade. They understood that when we were seventeen, we were only a year away from being on our own, so they wanted to make sure we were able to stand on our own two feet before we left the nest.

I often hear parents say, "As long as you're under my roof, you'll do what I say," and I've never understood it. If your kid is going to grow up and move out, don't you want him or her to have a smooth transition into the adult world? To me it seems logical that the way to do that is not to have tons of rules up until the day your kids leave, but to slowly cut back on your authority until they're independent.

WHEN RULES HINDER GENUINE FAITH

Something that seems to be common among Christian families is the tendency to use rules to try to ensure their children grow up to be good Christians. But what if the rules parents have about faith make their kids *less* likely to follow God?

That's what happened to Shiloh. In high school Shiloh was generally a good girl. "I had small, controlled rebellions," Shiloh giggled. "It was like I planned them. I'm a very safe person, so with everything I did, I made sure that I wouldn't be hurt in the long run. But I was not perfect at all—I dabbled in underage drinking, fought with my parents, and was really quite far from God. But if you ask my parents, I was perfect." On the computer screen where we were video chatting, I saw Shiloh's shoulders slump a bit. "They didn't know anything about that side of me."

Overall, looking at her track record, most people would see Shiloh's parents' methods of raising her as a major success. Their daughter is succeeding at college, volunteering at church, and in a healthy relationship with a great guy. However, Shiloh tells a different story.

"If you ask my parents," Shiloh told me, "they'd say I never rebelled, I was a good Christian, and they did everything right, because they still don't know about me drinking in high school or how much I struggled with my faith."

Shiloh grew up in a house with a lot of rules. Unlike Nathan's mom's rules, these rules didn't seem to be random—they were quite meticulous and consistent and were put in place to ensure that the children became good Christians. "Overall," Shiloh said, "I was extremely grateful to have parents who were very involved. However, there were a lot of times where they crossed a line and it seriously damaged our relationship. My biggest problem," Shiloh explained, "was that they never let me make my own decisions, not even with my faith. They would say that they trusted us to make the right decisions, but actions speak louder than words."

When I asked her to explain what she meant by that, Shiloh said, "Well, any time we had a chance to make a choice independently, they wouldn't let us. We had a rule that I wasn't allowed to date until I was eighteen. Then, when I was eighteen, a great Christian guy asked me out and I wanted to say yes. My parents liked the guy too. But instead of letting me make that choice for myself, my mom told me, 'No. You live in my house, so you have to listen to my rules, and I'm saying you can't date. And if you do go out with him, I'm not going to drive you to school anymore or make your meals, since you won't respect my rules.' All that did was make me resentful that I couldn't go out with him, even though I don't think it would have worked out in the end. I still should have been able to make that choice."

In Shiloh's family, rules served to allow her mom and dad to keep control over their kids. Most important, though, they allowed the parents to try to control their children's faith. "My family didn't have a strong spiritual base," Shiloh explained. "We didn't have a home church—we changed churches three times during my high school years alone. I think they were concerned about that, so they were trying to force religion on me. We had to be downstairs for breakfast by a certain time so we could have family devotions in the morning. We had to read a certain number of chapters from the Bible every day or we would lose our cell phones for a week. We even had rules about who prayed before each meal. God became part of the rules that I hated." Throughout high school Shiloh's relationship with God was rocky and not the strong, intimate bond with Christ that she wanted.

At the same time she was feeling insecure in her faith, when Shiloh was sixteen, she became friends with Sophia. "My friend Sophia came from a big Greek family," Shiloh told me, "and I used to go over to her house for family dinners. They were great—they were super involved in each other's lives and accepted each other just as they were. Sophia could tell her parents anything, and even if they were disappointed, the relationship stayed strong. Also, they really trusted her—they didn't hover over her shoulder or demand to know details about her life. Whenever I went to her house, I just thought, *Man, that's what I want with my family.* They weren't Christians, but they had so much love there."

It was at this family's house that she started to drink, since they were Greek and would routinely serve wine with dinner. The family without God seemed more joyous than her Christian family, and she wanted to be included in that joy. So, she drank with them, and that started a pattern of moderate underage drinking.

Fortunately, Shiloh had also stayed in touch with a girl she had met in church in the eighth grade. "Her name was Emma," Shiloh told me, "and she taught me to make my faith my own, just by watching how she lived and having conversations with her about her Jesus. If I hadn't met her, high school would have been very different for me. I already had a hard time keeping my faith strong, because often it seemed more like an obligation than a relationship. If it weren't for Emma, I truly believe I would have fallen away a long time ago and wouldn't be where I am now."

Today Shiloh is a human kinetics major and a leader of a Bible study with her on-campus Christian group. But Shiloh is strong in her faith *despite* all the strict rules she had growing up. The rules had worked to micromanage her faith, taking all the responsibility off her, never requiring her to actually make a decision concerning her walk with God. "I always knew that my parents really loved me." Shiloh sighed. "But I still don't feel that they trusted me, because I never got a chance to win their trust."

A common thread in several of the interviews I conducted was that Christians often turn faith into rules. The skating mom from the very beginning of this chapter, Shiloh's parents, even Megan's parents—they all saw faith as something they had to rigidly enforce. Now, Megan's family may not have succeeded well at the enforcement part, but nevertheless, the rules that Megan did have still revolved around Scripture. To me this seems counterintuitive.

I listened to all these stories, but I really had a difficult time understanding how a family could think that faith was about rules, because it was so opposite of how I was raised. At different times throughout my childhood and teenage years we'd try to have family devotions around the dinner table, but it seemed that somebody was always out of town or working, so the tradition could never get off the ground. Instead, Mom and Dad gave us Bibles and highlighters and let us loose to study for ourselves. We also didn't pray together on a regular basis, except before meals. I found it awkward to pray in front of my parents and Katie when it was a forced part of our routine. The times we did pray, it was for a reason. Daddy often called from work, telling us that he had a really sick premature baby or another sick child and that he needed us to pray. So we'd gather in the living room and all pray together for Dad's judgment and for the baby or child to pull through. But prayer was never scheduled.

In the families where kids always clung to faith, God was just a daily part of life. Our parents knew we had spiritual lives of our own. They knew we read our Bibles, kept prayer journals, and were able to foster our relationship with God independently. And we knew the same about them. Faith was simply a part of our family's culture. My mom used to remind us, "Children have the Holy Spirit as much as adults do. You are as capable of hearing His voice as anyone else." She trusted us to seek Him out on our own.

This focus on following the Spirit instead of following rules was found among every person I interviewed who didn't rebel. And a big area where our families turned to the Spirit instead of to rules was with Christian dating. The closest my family got to rules about dating was when my parents read *I Kissed Dating Goodbye*, by Joshua Harris, when I was thirteen and they decided that I shouldn't date until I was eighteen. By the time I was fifteen, however, they had completely abandoned that idea, realizing it was making Christianity more about following man-made rules than about following the Spirit. Instead of having strict rules about how or when or who to date, those of us who didn't rebel had rules like these:

- "Our parents tried to teach me and my sister that boys have cooties. After that didn't work, they talked to us about dating. There weren't rules. If it came up, we'd just talk about it. There weren't age limits. The only rule was that we had to run it by Mom and Dad first."

- "Sex wasn't something shameful in my family. It was a natural part of life that was meant for marriage, but it wasn't ever portrayed as bad or sinful. That openness is how my parents taught me that sexuality is healthy, but it's also why I chose to wait to have sex."

- "I originally wasn't supposed to date until I was eighteen, but I met the man I eventually married when I was only sixteen. I asked my mom if I could date him, and she said that I could. She explained that the only reason she was hesitant was that she was sorry I had met the right person too early—it's a long time to wait when you meet in high school!"

The problem with prescribed ideas of what faith *should* look like—such as the pressure to do family devotions, to pray together every night out loud, or to have strict rules about dating—is that they easily result in the same situation Shiloh dealt with. Faith becomes inauthentic because it becomes about rules, not about a relationship with God. Shiloh found that the rules around her faith stifled her ability to search out God for herself. It wasn't until someone introduced her to a faith outside of rules that she finally encountered Jesus.

WHY FAITH TRUMPS RULES

In Matthew 13 Jesus tells the parable of the sower. A sower goes out to plant his seeds, and some seeds end up on the rock, where they shoot up quickly but lack any root; some end up on the path, where birds snatch them away; some end up among thorns, where they are strangled by worry; but some end up on good soil, where they flourish and multiply. Obviously, the good soil is the option parents desperately want for their children. And often parents' ways of making sure their children are the good soil is by trying to micromanage faith using rules.

But what if rules don't actually work in creating good soil? Rules do not encourage personal growth. They merely dictate behavior. Shiloh didn't truly follow God until she met a friend who challenged her in high school to go beyond the rules and truly give her life to Christ, not just go through the motions. Megan came back to the faith after seeing the joy of Christians who were living by the Spirit contrasted with the rules-based religion her parents had tried to force on her. In both these cases, the girls became good soil by transcending the rules, not by following them. They became good soil despite the rules.

The rest of us who didn't rebel were raised not to follow rules for their own sake but to make good decisions, and that carried into our faith lives. Instead of trying to control our faith, my parents gave us independence. Their belief that we had the Holy Spirit as much as they did shaped how my parents raised us—instead of controlling us, they gave us freedom to make our own decisions, guided by our knowledge of Him. And through repeated practice, we learned discretion and how to identify when something was or was not from God. And that is how good soil was created in our lives.

Maybe the answer isn't to force kids to follow rules; maybe it's to allow them to hear from God themselves—even if that's scary and feels as though you're giving up control. If parents want their kids to have faith, then maybe parents need to start having some faith themselves that God can draw kids to Him, even without rules.

3

EXPECTATIONS

CHILDREN ARE A
SELF-FULFILLING PROPHECY

My best friend during elementary school was a girl named Monica. I was homeschooled and went to a church with only two other girls my age, so when I met Monica at Highland dancing lessons, we grew close very quickly. We talked on the phone, wrote stories together, and would stay up late during sleepovers, giggling about our junior high crush drama. Plus, she went to public school, which made her infinitely cool in my eyes. For little ten-year-old me, it was a pretty exciting time.

At her tenth birthday party, though, I suddenly realized how different we really were. After we sang "Happy Birthday" and Monica had blown out the candles, her mom remarked, "Only three more years until you're a teenager, and I'll have to be locking the windows at night to keep the boys out and you in!"

I remember thinking it very strange to even imagine that Monica would ever do something like sneak out to see a boy. She was a good kid and my friend—in my mind, it was just a given that we would be good kids forever. (I was still at the stage where, although I knew adulthood was part of my future, I couldn't picture a world where I wasn't a child.) But then I started to think about other things her mom used to say—things that seemed to encourage the idea that Monica and her brother were going to jump off the deep end as soon as they turned thirteen. I remembered her mother laughing when her kids rolled their eyes at her and showing Monica how to properly flip her hair with attitude as she stormed off from a fight—something my mom would have never allowed in a million years.

During high school Monica and I started going down very different paths. I was involved in Bible Quizzing (an international tournament program), and most of the friendships I pursued were from church. I researched what university I wanted go to. Monica dabbled in partying and the dating scene and watched movies and TV shows far more graphic than I was comfortable with. We no longer had anything but our history in common, but I still cared about her. During high school I found myself stuck, unable to help while I watched my friend slip further away and get her heart broken again and again, mostly as a result of her own behavior. She became the wild child; I stayed the good kid.

Expectations were obviously not the only thing to blame for her rebellion, but I remember how omnipresent that expectation of rebellion was in their house—and hearing little ten-year-old

Monica brag about what she'd be able to do when she was a teenager and her mother couldn't stop her.

In my family, on the other hand, rebellion was never expected. It wasn't even an option. Maybe it seems harsh, but my parents all but told us that teenage rebellion was just plain dumb, so we were never particularly tempted. In our minds drinking, drugs, partying, and listening to raunchy music equaled "dumb"—and I really didn't want to be dumb. Where most parents would say, "You're not allowed," my parents would say, "Don't be stupid." Instead of forbidding us to do things, they made those things shameful in our eyes. They expected more from us. They expected us to behave in a way that was God-honoring—in a way that would make our family and our future selves proud, and in a way that was wise. They expected this because they believed in our ability to make good choices. And because we knew they believed in us, we didn't want to let them down. In fact, it was such an omnipresent expectation that we wouldn't make regrettable choices that when my sister started her YouTube channel at age sixteen, the slogan she adopted was, "Don't be stupid or make bad decisions." Pretty much the mantra of the Gregoire house.

Research in psychology has shown that the amount of alcohol parents expect their children to drink can change the amount of alcohol their children actually drink.[1] If parents expect their kids to drink more, then the kids are more likely to drink more, and if they expect them to drink less, they drink less. When parents did not approve of alcohol use, teens "had fewer friends who drank and approved of drinking, greater self-efficacy for avoiding alcohol use, and less alcohol use and associated problems" than teens whose parents had less strong convictions against alcohol.[2]

But how does that work?

Picture this: A sixteen-year-old boy's parents are convinced he goes drinking with his friends after school, even though he's repeatedly assured them he has not. His parents don't believe him, though, because they believe that all teenagers try alcohol, so they constantly smell his breath, drill him about where he is, and refuse to let him have any freedom in case he goes and gets drunk.

One day, after a particularly bad fight with his parents, he and his friends are hanging out after school and one of the guys pulls out a six-pack. His parents already expect that he's drinking, and he's so hurt and frustrated with their mistrust of him that he doesn't care anymore and takes a beer. It is still his decision, but there are many factors playing into his behavior— including his parents' expectations.

When we as teenagers are expected to fail, it makes us feel as though we've messed up before we've even done anything wrong. Who our parents think we are shapes who we believe we are, which in turn becomes who we choose to be. In short, children will rise or fall according to their parents' expectations. The tragedy is that what our parents expect from us impacts our own self-image, and when our parents expect less than the best from us, we begin to believe we are worth less than our best, and that carries out in our actions. So, if expectations have such a huge impact on kids, why do parents keep expecting teenagers to fail?

I think that part of it is that the teenage years are hard for everyone. Going from kid to adult is a huge change, and no change goes completely smoothly. Even in families where the kids don't rebel, the teenage years can still be difficult. When I was a teenager, I didn't do anything particularly bad, but I was not exactly easy to live with. I got moody, I was melodramatic, and I fought with my sister.

For some parents, the teenage years are when their children are exposed for the first time to things that can be quite harmful, but teenagers can lack the emotional maturity to make the best decisions. So when they do rebel, it can often be quite extreme.

Thinking about this research triggered a memory from back when I was sixteen. One couple with kids in my youth group volunteered their house for a giant youth group summer kickoff. They were heavily involved in the church, so I talked with them over lunch since I knew them and we were friends. We started chatting about college, and the mother said, "Bet you can't wait to move out so you can just go find a boyfriend and move in with him. College is a crazy time."

Incredulous, I laughed and said, "No, of course I'm not going to move in with any boyfriend. Don't be silly!" I thought she was just teasing me. But I was proven wrong when the dad said, "That's what you think now, but then you'll get there, and watch—you'll get caught up in the college dating and party life just like everyone else."

I was shaken that a family so involved in the church could be so caught up in this idea that kids inevitably go off the rails. I can't help but look at their belief that it's impossible to stay out of the party scene in college and think, *What a waste.* Because you know what? It just isn't true. These kinds of false beliefs turn into expectations that impact the decisions kids make down the road—and it's a tragedy when teenagers and young adults fall away from their beliefs even partially because of something the people around them believed that turned out to be a lie.

But how do those expectations play themselves out in a good way? Let's take a look at Parker's and Alexis's stories to find out.

THE POWER OF EXPECTING SUCCESS

Parker and I have been best friends for years. We went to youth group together throughout high school. Parker is studying biomedical engineering. She's always been the good girl—the one the youth leaders love and parents hope their kids turn into when they grow up. One of the most striking things about her is her work ethic. She has always been a hard worker—you have to be to graduate with a biomedical engineering degree. According to Parker, a lot of her ability to buckle down and not get distracted by things other teens did, like partying, is because of her parents.

"My parents always said they wanted us to do our best for school," Parker explained when I asked her to expand on her parents' role, "but they were happiest when we got in the nineties with grades, because they knew we were capable of getting them. While they would say they were proud of us when we got lower than that"—Parker laughed—"they were never quite as excited as when we got those nineties."

Parker's parents expected their kids would value learning. When they were on vacation, they'd take Parker to museums or have her bring books instead of movies for car rides. They'd chat about what they were learning or what they saw and would listen and enjoy it when Parker got excited about some animal they saw at the zoo or an exhibit about Egyptian mummification rites. That started to shape Parker's self-concept—she saw herself as someone who was smart and who valued doing well at school. This led her to make decisions that would enable her to do her best academically, like choosing not to stay out late at night, staying in to complete her homework, and studying for tests.

Parker's family epitomized the "work hard, play hard" mantra. Not only did they have a great work ethic, they were also a lot of fun. Everyone knew that if you wanted to have a birthday party or a movie night, you wanted it to be at Parker's. Parker's parents would go all out—her mom would make the most amazing snacks, and her dad would get the pool ready for when friends came over. They had fun when friends weren't around too. Parker, her brother, and their parents would have dance parties in the living room, play games together, and go skiing or four-wheeling out in the woods whenever they could.

But her parents taught her that before you played, you had to get your work done, and you had to do it well. Then you could enjoy the good times even more. This wasn't just about homework, either. As Parker explained, "My parents praised us whenever we worked hard or did our best, and when they saw us not giving our all, we knew they expected more from us." Parker thought for a few seconds, then said, "It's hard to explain. We knew when they were disappointed, but they never dwelled on the negative. When we didn't try our best, my parents focused not on a list of the ways we had failed them but on how much more we could do if we just worked harder. Because they believed that we had so much potential, if we didn't give 100 percent they were disappointed—with cleaning, church, extracurricular activities, anything. But it was never a guilt trip; it was always a positive conversation about their faith that we could achieve greater things than when we only gave the bare minimum."

Aiming for the best also became the way Parker handled her faith. To Parker, God was always given 100 percent, and anything less was unacceptable and a waste of her potential—her parents taught her she was capable of more. In high school, this meant that she turned down party invitations, decided against dating non-Christians (despite having many offers), and became very involved with youth group and church. She found a house full of Christian roommates for her four years of college. She remained heavily involved in church and maintained Christian friendships as a priority, while many of her friends who had been strong in high school drifted away from their faith when they found themselves separated from their high school church friends.

Much of this success, according to Parker, is due to the healthy balance her parents struck between showing disappointment when Parker did not live up to what they knew she was capable of, and providing heaps of encouragement and involvement in her successes. They attended all her band performances, fussed over her art, and celebrated with her when she got a grade she needed. They kept her accountable in doing her homework and her chores, but they also had lots of fun and were silly together.

Now, it is easy to look at Parker's story and think, *Okay, but she's from the perfect Christian family. Of course she turned out fine. But what about with non-Christian households? Does the same rule apply?* Let's look at Alexis's story to see.

Alexis is currently in her second year of human kinetics and also didn't rebel during her high school years. She never got involved in binge drinking, drugs, sex, or slacking off in school, like other kids did. When she was in the eleventh grade, she was permitted to go to some parties and drink, but always in moderation, and she was expected to be smart about it. "My parents wanted me to make good decisions," Alexis explained, "so whenever I went out they needed to be told ahead of time, and they gave me clear guidelines as to what was responsible or irresponsible drinking."

When she did not live up to their expectations, Alexis knew it. "My parents were constantly telling me how much they trusted me, and I felt so horrible and disappointed in myself if I ever abused the rules they enforced," Alexis explained. "Also, they would have felt betrayed after all the support they had given me throughout my life. My parents raised me to make good decisions on my own. They constantly told me that they knew I was 'smarter than that' when I would talk about other people at school who were partying, drinking, sleeping around, and the like."

It's funny how the parents of kids who didn't rebel, when trying to teach their kids how to make good decisions, focused on whether the act was smart or stupid instead of right or wrong. Of course, there was always a moral element, but for the most part the expectations all our parents had for us revolved around what was a smart choice versus what would hurt us in the long run.

- My parents told us, "Why would you want to do that? That's dumb."
- Parker's parents told her, "We expect you to know better."
- Alexis's parents said, "You're smarter than that."

All our parents expected us to make the right choices because they knew we wouldn't make dumb ones.

Alexis's parents made those expectations clear in two main ways: open communication and acknowledgment of success. Her parents were active in talking about hard issues such as sex, drugs, and partying. When she was going into the ninth grade, they talked to Alexis about issues she would face in high school. "They wanted to make sure that I heard about this stuff from them first," Alexis explained, "because they knew that otherwise I'd be getting my information from the kids at school. They wanted to make sure there was openness concerning these topics so that I didn't feel any desire to experiment behind their backs."

Since Alexis is naturally very introverted, it was helpful for her that her parents initiated this open communication. "With my personality type," Alexis said, laughing, "if they had never made those conversations happen, we probably wouldn't have ever talked about it. But the fact that they forced those conversations to happen and drove that information into my head made all the difference."

Alexis's parents always praised her when she met their expectations as well. They frequently told her they were proud of her when she had worked hard at school, was responsible at work, or made good decisions in her personal life. "My moral judgments grew so strong," Alexis explained, "that it was no longer about not disappointing my parents but about the impact that rebellious actions would have on me and on my future. I didn't want rebellious acts to become habits that became who I was."

According to Alexis, her parents' hopes for her made such an impact partly because they were reasonable and led to things that Alexis also wanted for herself. "My parents did push their expectations on me, but they were all expectations that, if I achieved them, would make me happy too. To do well in school, go to university, stay away from drugs and sex—it's clear how they benefited me."

Sometimes parents can get into a rut of only communicating the times they are disappointed with their kids and forget to encourage the small victories, like doing a great job at cleaning the toilet. No matter how good expectations are, they need to be communicated with a balance of positive and negative feedback. But what happens when kids only hear about their parents' disappointment?

THE DAMAGE OF EXPECTING FAILURE

As I thought about Parker, Alexis, and Monica, I also started thinking about Hailey. Hailey's story is different from the others'.

WHY I DIDN'T REBEL

Like Monica's mom, Hailey's mom expected rebellion. However, while Monica's mom just gave up and accepted the "fact" that her child was going to rebel, Hailey's mom did the opposite. Hailey's mom took it one step further, actively distrusting Hailey even when she wasn't rebelling.

Hailey's parents divorced when she was eight, and her dad moved to the other side of the country for work. So Hailey, not wanting to leave her friends, ended up living with her mother. When she was twelve her mother met a man we'll call Carl. They married three years later. When I asked her about her relationship with her mother, I was saddened by her reply.

"I can count the number of times my mom has said she was proud of me on one hand," Hailey told me, "but I couldn't tell you how many times she told me she was disappointed or that I had failed." In fact, when I asked her which were her best memories with her mom, she said that they were when she was skating— her mom went to all her competitions and cheered her on, and it was the only time Hailey heard that her mom was proud of her.

Hailey would confront her mom at times and say, "Are you ever proud of me?" and her mother would reply, "Oh, I'm always proud of you." However, Hailey always felt that it was a cover-your-bases kind of answer, since her mom's actions day-to-day showed the exact opposite.

The major problem between Hailey and her mother was that her mother assumed Hailey had done something wrong even when she had not. What really threw a wrench in their relationship was Hailey's stepdad, who from Hailey's perspective deliberately undermined her. Many times her stepdad would say that Hailey had done something she had not, and her mother would trust her husband over her daughter. For example, once Hailey was nursing a skating injury while participating in a fund-raising event for the rink. She had caught laryngitis from some girl on the league, and she had forgotten some supplies at the house, about two blocks away. She was on crutches, so she asked Carl if he could grab the supplies. He said sure and went to get them.

About five minutes later Hailey got a phone call from her mom, who screamed at her, saying, "How could you have done that? You can't yell at Carl and order him around in front of your friends! You need to apologize to him right now in front of all of your friends for yelling at him and disrespecting him like that!"

Hailey, flabbergasted, replied, "I've lost my voice! I couldn't have yelled at him if I wanted to!" However, since she expected Hailey to be dishonest and disrespectful, her mom stood by Carl's story and required an apology from Hailey. So Hailey apologized, although all the people who had witnessed it thought the apology was unnecessary.

Hailey's high school experience was rough. During her freshman year she was bullied so much that she wouldn't stay at school during lunch, but had her mom pick her up every day to go home and eat. By tenth grade she had finally made some friends—but they were from a bad crowd. She descended into the party scene, experimented with drugs, and started having sex. In grades eleven and twelve she started lying to her mom about everything. She snuck out to parties, got into fights, and kept going down a path she, with the benefit of hindsight, admits was self-destructive. "My mom already thought I was a horrible kid," Hailey said, "so what was the point anymore? All I wanted to do from tenth grade on was leave, but I couldn't."

When you hear Hailey talk about her high school experience, though, you don't hear a jaded story about how terrible her mom was. Rather, you hear a story of hurt and confusion, but also of grace. When Hailey's mom was a teenager, she had rebelled. A lot. So as Hailey approached high school age, her mom got scared that her little girl would follow the same destructive path she had. Unfortunately, her fear-based parenting resulted in mistrust between the two of them. That mistrust led Hailey to seek out friends who would believe in her, since she felt her mother didn't. These friends ended up being the kids from the party crowd.

"They seemed real—they had my back through thick and thin, didn't talk behind my back, and didn't assume that any rumors they heard about me were true," Hailey explained, when I asked her why she became so close with the kids in the "bad" crowd. "Whenever they heard someone spreading rumors about me, they would come to me first and ask if it was true instead of just immediately believing that it was." Hailey's friends at school, although they were into partying and drugs, gave her something she wasn't getting at home—an expectation that she would do the right thing. They trusted that she would be honest with them, and they were honest with her in return.

Now, there is nothing wrong with expressing disappointment to a child. My parents were not shy in telling us when we had done something to disappoint them, and not wanting to disappoint them again motivated us to do the right thing next time. But unlike my sister and me, Hailey *only* heard about the disappointment; Hailey's mom didn't tell her when she had met or surpassed her expectations, and it created confusion for Hailey. "When I was fourteen or so," Hailey recalled, "I thought I was fine—I never knew what I had done to make her so angry at me."

When I asked her one thing she thought could have changed it all, she said, "Kids need positive feedback from their parents. They just do—kids deserve to know when their parents are proud of them."

FEAR- AND FAITH-BASED PARENTING

Looking at all these stories, I saw a pattern emerging: families who expected their kids to rebel were scared, and families who didn't expect their kids to rebel had a lot of faith in their children. Parker's and Alexis's parents both trusted them and knew they could make the right decisions. Monica's and Hailey's moms both reacted to the teenage years the same way: out of fear. Each was just waiting for the moment her child became some teenage monster. The difference lay in what each did with that fear; Monica's mom gave up while Hailey's mom tried to crack down with rules in an attempt to curb that inevitable rebellion.

This made me think back to the people I interviewed in the rules chapter—especially Shiloh. Her mom had tons of rules because she didn't trust her children to make the right decisions. She also expected rebellion from her kids and used rules to try to control what she saw as their inescapable rebellion. She was parenting out of fear, not out of faith in her kids.

This mind-set seems to be quite common. An expectation that children will rebel leads to frantic measures to stop that rebellion, which then take the form of extreme numbers of rules. As I pondered this, I called my sister to talk to her about it (because I'm pretty much incapable of thinking through anything on my own). She started laughing and told me about an e-mail she had received a few weeks before from one of her YouTube viewers. It said:

> My three-year-old daughter won't stop taking her clothes off. No matter what I try, she just rips them off. How can I teach my three-year-old what it means to be modest, and that God made parts of her body for only her and her future husband?

"I'm sorry, but *what?*" I said to Katie, incredulous. Sure, parents need to help kids keep clothes on, but does a three-year-old really need a lesson on modesty? I felt for this mother, because if this was something she was concerned about, the rest of her daughter's childhood was not going to be easy.

As with Hailey and Shiloh, an inherent fear showed in that e-mail. Shiloh's mom couldn't see that Shiloh was capable of choosing to date the right person. Hailey's mom was so scared she couldn't differentiate between when Hailey did or did not do something wrong. This mom was afraid her daughter was being immodest when in reality she was just being three. With this mom, it seemed there was a fear that "If I don't enforce all these strict rules, my child will go off the deep end."

"Lots of young children hate wearing clothes! That's the part I don't get," Katie said. "How worried she is over something normal. I mean, I don't think we have a single home video of me where I'm fully dressed until I'm around four or five years old!"

"Yeah," I teased. "But to be fair, the fact that you did it, too, really doesn't mean it's normal." Although she wasn't particularly concerned about the streaking, Mom did teach Katie to wear her clothes when she was outside, because for a while we lived across the street from a pedophile on house arrest.

But that's what this fear-based parenting style does—it blinds parents from seeing what their kids are actually experiencing in the present. This mom was making her child's disrobing a moral issue when in reality it just wasn't. When a three-year-old is streaking, you don't teach modesty—you just teach the child how to wear clothes. Discussions about modesty can come later. Let's be honest: a lot of times it's just a lot more fun to run around naked than in a bunch of restricting clothes. But by making it a modesty issue, this mom could start to shame a child for simply liking how the breeze feels on her bum.

Erik Erikson is a psychologist who proposed a model of children's development and revolutionized developmental psychology. His model is based around the crises that each age faces. For example, from birth until about the first year, the main crisis a child faces is trust versus mistrust. *Will my needs be taken care of? Is the world one that I can trust, or do I have no certainty in my life?* If the baby's needs are met and the people in its life are caring and predictable, the baby begins to foster hope, which is the basis of the confidence needed for autonomous behavior later.[3]

In the toddler years, where the child in the previous e-mail would have been, the main crisis is autonomy versus shame and doubt.[4] The child is old enough to move away from the parent a bit and explore on his or her own but is still very young and needs the parent to provide structure to and protection for the exploration. However, it's hard to strike a balance between encouraging the child's curiosity and protecting the child from potential harm. Chastising this exploration too harshly can lead to shaming the child. Too much shame for a young child can be harmful and can sometimes lead children to be defiant and shameless.[5] This is why, when dealing with young children especially, it's important not to be governed by fear. The child needs a healthy mix of freedom and structure and to be encouraged to explore the world without having adult problems projected onto a child's innocent behaviors.

My family, along with Parker's family, wasn't particularly afraid of anything. Instead, our families were rooted in faith. Alexis's parents, although not Christian, had faith that their children would make good decisions because the parents were wise people. My mom and dad had faith that we would make good decisions because of what they believed about God. My mom would tell me, "Why shouldn't I expect you to make good decisions? I expect myself to make good decisions, so why wouldn't I expect the same of you when we have the same Holy Spirit inside of us?"

Last Sunday my church had a service in the local park. We had three babies dedicated that Sunday, beneath the trees with birds chirping. In the dedication the parents promised to raise their children up to know God, and the prayer given was that they would grow up to make the right choices and to live with God in their hearts forever. Somehow, it's easy to be filled with faith when children are young, but it's like we forget, when the kids turn into teenagers, to maintain that trust.

EXPECTATIONS: A SELF-FULFILLING PROPHECY

Self-fulfilling prophecy is a term for when you believe something so much that it makes you behave in a way that makes it come true. If you hadn't believed that thing, though, it might never have happened. For example, you have a social event, and you believe you're going to be awkward and everyone will think you are strange. So when you get there, you're nervous and a little jumpy and you say things you probably shouldn't, and some people think you're a little strange . . . because you're so worried about people thinking that you are strange. The same thing happens with how we expect kids to behave.

Because of her parents' expectations, rebellion seemed like a natural part of growing up to Monica. It seemed like the mature thing to do, since it was treated as a rite of passage in her home: First time you sneak out to make out with a boy. First high school party. First time throwing up because you've had too much beer. These were all landmarks along the path to adulthood. Naturally, when she hit her teenage years and desperately wanted to grow up, like every teenager, Monica followed the path put before her.

In Hailey's case, her mom expected that she had been disrespectful, had lied, and had generally been a horrible kid. So, Hailey began to think it wasn't worth it anymore to try to do right.

The great news is that the flip side is also true. We see this with Parker, Alexis, and me—all of whom had parents who believed their kids *would* behave well and make good choices. We had parents who ran a faith-based family. We received praise and recognition for doing well not only in things like sports or academics but in personal virtues as well. We felt our parents believed in us and that they expected greatness because they thought we were capable of it. And you know what? We're all really grateful to our parents for believing in us. The teenage years are hard for kids as they're going through them. Having a parent who has your back and believes in you can make all the difference.

4

COMMUNICATION

LET'S TALK ABOUT TALKING

When Courtney was a child, her family members were her closest friends. There was constant chatter in their house; Courtney gabbed with her mom about all her crushes, her favorite books, her drama with friends—everything.

But Courtney's family, although very close, struggled with mental-health issues. Her dad was bipolar, her mom was depressed, Courtney had anxiety, and her little brother had ADHD and anger management issues. None of the mental-health issues were being treated, but for many years the family held things together pretty well.

Everything changed, though, when in Courtney's sixth-grade year her grandmother died. The grandmother had unified the family, and her death came as a shock to everyone. Now, on top of her own depression and her son's frequent angry outbursts, Courtney's mother was dealing with grieving the loss of her mother.

All of this didn't leave any time for meaningful communication with her daughter. "My mom thought she knew everything about me." Courtney shrugged. "But she never knew what was actually going on. I so wanted to be able to talk to her about Grandma, but whenever I wanted to, she was too busy or just couldn't handle it."

Courtney felt her grandmother's death acutely, as the two were especially close. "I couldn't talk about my grief," Courtney explained, "because my mom was always so busy with my brother. I had a hard time talking about it in the first place, and when I was finally ready to open up, my mom would sit down with me, and then five minutes in my brother would throw another fit." By the time her mom had finished dealing with her brother, Courtney felt she had been abandoned in a time of need and closed up again.

"I started feeling really resentful," Courtney explained, "because I saw my brother taking all my mom's time so I couldn't even talk to her, but she didn't do anything to help him get better. It was all crisis management—there was zero treatment for my brother." So Courtney had to deal with her grief and anxiety alone.

In high school Courtney's mom made her go to counseling for a short time to try to deal with her anxiety problems and grief. It was a flop. "On my last session," Courtney recalled, "I told the counselor, 'I'm not coming back. This isn't helping.' The counselor told me, 'If you stopped trying to railroad every question I asked, maybe talking about it would help.' I just laughed and said, 'I don't want to talk about it with you—I want to talk about it with my mom. No matter what you say, you can't fix the fact that I can't talk about it with my mom because my mom isn't here.'"

By age sixteen Courtney had been dealing with anxiety, unresolved grief, and resentment toward her brother and mom for five years. Craving that closeness she had wanted with her mom, she turned to boys. "I had an unfortunate dating streak in high school," Courtney said. "I was just looking for a real connection in all the wrong places, and I got really hurt because of it."

This dating caused even more of a rift between Courtney and her mother. Eventually things got so bad at home that Courtney decided to move out and rent from family friends. "Moving out was a really hard decision," Courtney told me, "but at the time I didn't feel I had any other choice. I was watching my family and myself fall apart, and I couldn't talk to anyone about it. I felt that I was the problem that was making my family crumble. So I left when I was only sixteen.

"When I moved out," Courtney said, "I remember my mom said, 'Why are you hurting us like this? Now I'm going to have to deal with your brother being upset because you're gone. You're being selfish.' And I was livid." Courtney shook her head. "Even my moving out was about my brother. My mom didn't ask me what I was feeling that made me think I needed to leave. All I wanted was for her to notice that I needed help too. To feel like I was as important to her as my brother was."

Courtney did find someone who put her first, and now she is happily married, living far from her family, and creating her own life away from the chaos. Looking back on her rocky relationship with her family, Courtney's face fell. "Leaving was the best thing for my own mental stability, but I missed out on so much with my family. I missed a whole two years with them, and that's something I can never get back." She shrugged. "I didn't want to leave. I just wanted to be heard."

COMMON THEMES AMONG PARENTS WHO COMMUNICATE WELL

I feel so much for Courtney, and I'm so glad that my experience was nothing like hers. My family has always talked about everything, not just the superficial stuff. Sure, we talked about boys and clothes and high school drama (well, I talked about boys with my mom—my dad learned about all of it later from her because most fourteen-year-old girls don't want to chat with Daddy about which boys they think are cute). But we also talked about my struggles and my spiritual walk on a regular basis. Even since I've moved out, I still FaceTime my mom and dad every day (generally whenever I'm folding laundry, making dinner, or trying to distract myself from my responsibilities, and right when my mom is trying to get actual work done). I know that sounds crazy, but you simply can't overestimate how extroverted my family is. We stop talking, we die.

Probably the greatest similarity among all the families I interviewed with kids who didn't rebel is that the kids felt they could talk to their parents about everything and anything. Among kids who did rebel, though, not one said that they could talk to their parents about what they were honestly feeling. Not one.

Getting teenagers to want to be honest with parents can be frustrating. Teens are constantly texting and video chatting and hanging out with friends, but when it comes to talking to parents, teens can seem to completely shut down.

However, just because it's frustrating doesn't mean it's impossible. I've found some common themes among families who communicate well versus those who do not. Families with good communication all used specific tools for communication: respect for their child's privacy, active listening, and ritualized communication spaces.

RESPECTING PRIVACY: GETTING MORE INFORMATION BY ASKING FOR LESS

Remember Hailey, whose mom was so scared that Hailey would do something bad that she started to read rebellion into her daughter's every move, even when her daughter wasn't rebelling at all? Because she was so sure that Hailey would make bad choices, Hailey's mom felt she needed to know everything going on in her daughter's life, even if that meant going behind her back.

"When I was in ninth grade," Hailey told me, "my relationship with my mom wasn't great, but at least we still talked." She would come home from school and have lunch with her mom every day, and although they fought quite a bit, at least they still had some time where they talked about what was going on in Hailey's life. "I wouldn't say we had a *good* relationship then," Hailey explained, "but it wasn't *terrible*. The definite breaking point didn't come until my sophomore year of high school."

When Hailey was in tenth grade, her mom went through

her phone and read her texts. After she found out that Hailey had gone to a party, she was so angry that she yelled at her and snapped her phone in half. Hailey was furious. "That was the end of our relationship," Hailey told me. "Knowing that she went behind my back and snooped in my phone, even though I really was doing some bad stuff, it completely broke my trust in her." Even though her mom had a reason to pry—she was scared her daughter was doing something unwise—the way she went about getting the information irreversibly damaged their relationship.

But how can parents get kids to tell them things and still respect their privacy? It might feel like a one-or-the-other option. From my interviews, though, it seems that respecting kids' privacy is one of the best ways to get them to talk to you. I know that sounds counterintuitive, but it's true. Here are some examples:

- "I felt like I had a lot of privacy, but I chose to share things anyway. A big part of our relationship was that when I didn't want to share something, my parents respected that and let me have some space. They didn't pressure me, but still made it very clear that they wanted to be involved in my life. So when I did want to talk about it, I always knew I could go to them."

- "I'm introverted, so I didn't always tell my parents the details about my life. I gave them more of a general overview and didn't go into specifics unless I felt that it was important. My parents gave me a bit of pressure in terms of details, because they knew that I'm not naturally talkative, but it was never overwhelming. If I said I didn't want to talk about it and could give a good reason why, they dropped it. In general, I was really open with them, and I was glad they gave me the freedom to decide when to disclose."

- "I shared a lot with my dad, but I shared everything with my mom. For as long as I can remember, I've just told them everything, since we've always talked all the time. But they never pushed for information, and when they asked me how I was doing, it wasn't an interrogation. I knew it was because they honestly wanted to know how I was doing."

But how do you get to a place with your children where respecting their privacy makes them want to share more? How do you encourage that kind of open, free-flowing communication? Samantha's story might help us understand how.

No Reason to Keep Secrets

Samantha was a good kid—she excelled in school, never got into the party scene as a teen, and connected with Christian groups on campus when she moved to university. She married her high school sweetheart and generally made good choices. When I asked Samantha to tell me some words that describe her relationship with her parents, she said quickly, "Honesty and openness, 100 percent."

Interestingly, when I asked Samantha how her parents created such an open space for communication, one reason she gave was by respecting her privacy. But this was a trick that was learned from experience. "My older brothers just wouldn't communicate once they became teenagers," Samantha explained.

"It was a constant battle. My parents tried to force my brothers to tell them things, like their grades or where they were going, but it just made it worse. So by the time they got to my sister and me, they had changed their strategy. Now they said, 'Tell us what you want. We're here—no pressure to divulge anything you don't want to tell us.'" Since there was no threat that Samantha's privacy would be taken away, there was no need to be defensive about keeping secrets from her parents.

But if you're never forcing your children to tell you *some* things, how do you make it likely that they'll tell you *any*thing at all? The way Samantha's parents did it was by ensuring honesty was never punished. Respecting privacy has two parts: allowing a child to disclose what he or she decides to disclose, and then encouraging disclosure to make it more likely to happen again. Otherwise, you just seem kind of aloof—as if you don't care whether or not your kids tell you anything.

"There was one night," Samantha recalled, "when my sister was in high school that she called our parents and said, 'I'm drunk and I need to come home. Can you come and get me?' My parents were *really* against underage drinking, but they didn't scream at her over the phone. Instead, my dad drove to the party, picked her up, and brought her home and let her go to bed." The next morning, Samantha's sister had to sit down for a discussion about what had happened, but there was no screaming, no grounding, no cell phone taken away. When Samantha asked her mom why, her mom told her, "We couldn't get mad at her because she called us, told us what was happening, and was honest. Getting mad would not have helped." They definitely did not approve of the situation, and they made that very clear. But Samantha's parents knew that if they had gotten angry with their daughter when she decided to open up, she would be less likely to open up in the future.

Seeing her mom grateful that her children would tell her the truth, even if it was an ugly one, made Samantha more likely to tell her mom her own secrets. "I wasn't afraid to tell my parents anything," Samantha said, "because we were never punished for opening up."

As a result, when Samantha's friends started to get into the party scene, she felt free to talk to her mom about what was going on instead of experimenting for herself. "Any time I went out," Samantha explained, "I'd come home after and sit down in this one spot in our living room while my mom sat in her chair, and we'd just talk about everything. When my friends were getting into drinking and partying, often my mom knew about it before their parents did."

No one wants to talk to someone who is prying for more information. It's uncomfortable, and you feel violated. Likewise, the people I talked to who disclosed the most to their parents felt that their parents pried the least. The more parents pried, the less their kids wanted to talk to them.

Trust and Respect

Communication is, in essence, about two things: trust and respect. You're only going to tell someone a secret or confide in him or her if (a) you trust that he or she will not judge you and (b) you know the person respects you enough not to blab it to everyone else or trivialize what you're going through. When parents pry or go behind their kids' backs to get information, as Hailey's mom did, it says, "I do not trust you to make good decisions, and I don't respect your privacy." That doesn't set up a climate where a kid wants to be honest with his or her mom or dad.

On the other hand, when you respect your children's privacy, it shows they can trust you to not overstep and that you respect their decision-making capabilities. It also shows them that you trust they will come to you with important things and that you trust them to be able to tell what kinds of things they need to tell you and what kinds of things are fine to keep to themselves. That's what Samantha's family did, as did all the other families of kids who didn't rebel that I interviewed.

ACTIVELY LISTENING

When Connor and I got married, we participated in premarital counseling. One of the exercises was a lesson in how to listen. I thought, *That's stupid—everyone knows how to listen.* But I proved myself wrong.

The exercises revealed that often, when I talked to Connor, instead of actively being present and listening to what he was saying, I was running through the groceries I needed to buy that night. Or, when we were arguing, I was planning my next rebuttal. In addition, I learned, as did Connor, that we are both guilty of minimizing the problems the other is experiencing when we offer a simple solution without truly empathizing with our spouse's pain.

When we speak to our spouses, we know we need to be attentive, nonjudgmental, and nondefensive. This allows us to really hear what they're saying instead of minimizing it, like when I was thinking about groceries instead of listening to what Connor was saying. But my interviews revealed that parents, when they talk to their kids, often forget the importance of actively listening. Lila's story shows one example.

Lila's parents divorced when she was in elementary school. From the outside their divorce looked like a "healthy" one—Lila had consistent rules between the households, the parents weren't in open conflict, and Lila did well in school. However, when I asked about her experience growing up, Lila said, "Although I could talk to my parents about superficial things, I couldn't talk to them about things that mattered, like the divorce. My dad was unwilling to get into an emotional conversation, and if I brought it up with Mom, it would become a huge fight where she would accuse me of blaming her for my problems." Lila shrugged. "They really did love me, but after enough of those fights, I just stopped going to them with my problems."

This put strain on Lila. Even though her parents loved her, their inability to let down their defenses and allow Lila to openly discuss her grief about the separation was toxic to their relationship. "Thankfully," Lila said with a smile, "I found a youth group in high school that became my support that I was missing in my parents. Without them, I would not be so involved in my faith now. They gave me a place to be heard, understood, and accepted."

Despite being in a good place thanks to her walk with Christ, Lila still mourns the missed opportunity of having a great relationship with her mom and dad. By not taking the time to properly process what was happening to a point where they could openly listen to their child's experience, her parents robbed Lila of a strong relationship with either of them. Lila's mom made the separation something Lila had to go through alone.

The Importance of Self-Care

Lila's story is very similar to Courtney's, and for one particular reason: both of these families failed to deal with barriers to communication with their children. With Courtney's family it was the mental-health issues running rampant in the house. With Lila it was her parents' ability—or lack of ability—to cope with the divorce. Neither set of parents was putting in the time to deal with their own issues, so they were unable to actively listen to their children.

Unfortunately, many parents do not deal with their mental-health or emotional issues. According to the World Health Organization (WHO), one in four people struggle with a mental illness, but fewer than two-thirds of people with a mental illness seek treatment.[1] So Courtney's family is not an anomaly. And tragically, mental-health issues that are not treated can lead to dysfunctional families. Children of parents with psychological difficulties are more likely to lack social skills normal for their age,[2] exhibit problematic behavior,[3] and have less open communication with their parents.[4] Much of this may happen because when parents experience mental-health issues, they are often less positive, less warm, and less engaged in their parenting.[5]

A professor of mine who specialized in family psychology once said, "Parenting is like being on an airplane in an emergency—if the oxygen masks fall, you have to put yours on first before assisting anyone else. It's the same with your kids: you can't help them unless you help yourself first." Courtney didn't feel that she could go to her mom because her mom hadn't taken care of her own issues first and because Courtney's brother hadn't received the treatment he needed. Courtney, then, was never truly heard. Lila's parents hadn't properly coped with the grief that comes with divorce. As a result, her mom was unable to discuss her daughter's experience without feeling attacked. And Lila missed out on having a mom who truly knew who she was.

Showing Them They're Worth Your Time

Teenagers are just like everyone else: they just want to be heard, understood, and accepted. To do that, they need their parents to actively listen, to be completely present in the conversation. Being 100 percent present doesn't mean you need to be sitting down on the couch, like in a therapist's office, but it does mean that your mind is solely focused on your child, even if you're doing something like driving or washing dishes. Similar to how you wouldn't want your child to have his or her phone out at the dinner table, your child doesn't want to feel as if you have more important things to do than talk to him or her. Active listening shows us teens that you find us interesting and that we aren't an inconvenience. We're worth setting aside a time of your day when we have 100 percent of your attention.

Effective parents actively listen. My parents were great at this—not only with me, but with my friends too. They would ask us questions that required more than just yes or no answers and would actually start a conversation. Questions like, "How do you like your new job?" or "What do you think about [recent news]?" They asked me questions that allowed them to see more than just the outside shell of who I was—they wanted to know what I was thinking and how I was feeling. They made it a priority to give me time to discuss what I was struggling with in my faith, and it really strengthened our relationship.

Active listening was such a habit for my parents that they didn't stop with Katie and me. Throughout high school I constantly had friends telling me, "Man, I wish I had your parents" or asking, "Can't your family just adopt me already?" I used to think they were crazy, because even though I had a great relationship with them, I still thought my parents were pretty embarrassing and that my friends' parents seemed so much cooler. But when I talk to the friends I knew in high school now, they all remember my parents the same way. My parents actually heard them because they treated them as though they were unique and special rather than just another teen. This really stood out to the five friends I asked—that's pretty big considering that as a homeschooler I didn't have very many close friends in high school.

Making Communication a Priority

Frankly, though, active listening isn't always easy—especially when you're a busy family. That was the barrier Liam and Paul's family had to cross.

Liam and Paul are great guys and always have been. And neither of the brothers ever rebelled. "My relationship with my parents has always been super strong," Liam explained. "So even though later in high school there were a few isolated incidents where I disobeyed my parents, I never really rebelled. I didn't want to let them down." Paul's opinion was much the same.

The brothers' dad, Derek, fostered a strong relationship with each of his sons by making sure he had time to talk with them individually. Now, this wasn't an easy task—Derek worked an extremely physically demanding job that required long hours and often nights spent away from home. When he did get home at the end of the day, he was exhausted. Nevertheless, making moments with his sons was a priority, and he took time consistently to get away with Liam and Paul.

"We went on hunting trips every year," Paul explained, "and we just sat and talked for hours as we waited for deer. Not too loudly, of course, so we didn't scare any off. Sometimes Liam would go out with him; then I'd go out, or we'd all go, the three of us. It was just a great chance to catch up with how we were all doing."

In addition to the hunting trips, Derek regularly made time for his sons throughout the week, despite his nonstop, ridiculous hours. "No matter how tired he was," Liam told me, "he always saw family as his first priority. So we'd go for a hike together to talk about the day or get a great fire going in the winter. He always had time for us, and time where we could just talk too. We knew that we were important to him."

Like Liam and Paul, those of us who didn't rebel felt that our parents were truly interested in what we had to say. They were really listening, and not just so they could defend themselves, as Lila's mom did. They took time out of their day when they shut out the rest of the world and just talked to us; they dealt with the barriers to communication that we faced, like a hectic family schedule.

Respecting privacy is step one to communication with teens. It tells them, "I respect and trust you." Active listening is step two. It says, "I like you and find you interesting." Step three is where it all comes together.

RITUALIZED COMMUNICATION SPACES

Respecting privacy, and therefore telling your teen that you trust and respect him or her, may encourage open communication. Actively listening may foster meaningful communication, but how do you get the conversation started in the first place?

According to my interviews, the answer is *ritualized communication spaces*—places or situations that are set apart so communication can happen routinely. For our family, it was our hot tub. My parents bought it when I turned fourteen. I thought they got it because they wanted a hot tub (who wouldn't?), but I later learned there were some ulterior motivations. One of my mom's friends had five boys, the youngest of whom was my age. This friend had gone through the teenage years just before my mom had to, and her number-one piece of advice: "Buy a hot tub. Teens get in there and they just spill everything."

And you know what? That is 100 percent true. There is something about just sitting together, with nothing else to do, in a relaxed environment that leads to sharing and easy communication. The hot tub became the place where Katie and I talked to Mom and Dad about everything—from boys to school to fights with friends. It was our space where we talked so often that soon talking just became a natural part of the hot tub experience. I quickly picked up on that and started inviting friends over to the hot tub if I knew they needed to talk about something. It worked without fail.

All but one of the people that I talked to who didn't rebel had a similar experience throughout their teenage years. Maybe not a hot tub per se, but there always seemed to be a place or a time that was just "the talking space." It was a routine where communication had happened so often before that, when you went there, you became almost primed to want to talk about what you were going through. That's why I call them ritualized communication spaces.

Here are some examples I found when I was interviewing people:

- For Samantha, it was grocery shopping. They lived half an hour from town, so when she and her mom went grocery shopping they had the car ride there, the shopping time, and the car ride back. "It just always seemed to happen—even if I didn't want to talk, by halfway into town I was telling Mom everything that had happened that day."
- Amanda had a spot in the living room where she sat and talked to her mom every afternoon as she got home from school. Her mom was always waiting for her, coffee in hand, ready to hear about her day.
- For Heidi, it was the dinner table. "Every dinner we would sit down and have an honest discussion about how we were each doing; it was time that we knew was meant for catching up with each other and really talking, not just chatting."

Setting aside a time or a place for real communication made talking about real issues more natural for all of us. It became a routine that we were used to, so when a big issue came up, we already knew how and when to come to Mom or Dad, and it wasn't awkward or forced.

The big thing about ritualized communication spaces is that it gave communication a natural "on" switch in our relationships. We knew that no matter what happened, we'd always get a chance to talk when we went into the hot tub or on a car trip or when we sat down for dinner. It gave us a sense of certainty and reassurance that our parents wanted to talk to us, and that there would be a time and a place whenever we needed it.

COMMUNICATION IS ABOUT CONNECTING

What families who communicated effectively got right was making communication a time to truly connect with the children. Families with ineffective communication didn't get that. There was something in the way of truly connecting, be it mental-health issues, guilt, or fear.

For those of us who didn't rebel, it was quite the opposite. We always knew that our parents truly wanted to hear what we had to say, so they did anything they could to encourage us to come to them when we needed to talk. They wanted to know what we were feeling, even when it was hard for them to hear, so they actively listened to us and gave us their full attention. Wanting communication to be routine, they helped develop ritualized communication spaces so that connecting became a natural part of our relationship. But the end goal wasn't getting information—it was getting to know us. It was a real relationship so that, unlike Courtney, we didn't have to search elsewhere to find someone who wanted to listen. We were heard and accepted right where we were.

5

FRIENDSHIP

GIVING KIDS A PLACE TO BELONG

When I was sixteen I worked as a lifeguard at the local YMCA. I loved it—it was the best job I've ever had. My boss even came to my wedding. One of the things I enjoyed the most, though, was just hanging out with my coworkers.

The high school students who work at a YMCA as lifeguards and swimming teachers tend to be the good kids. They are usually the kids who have been involved in swimming lessons and then choose to put in the work to become lifeguards at only sixteen. They're responsible and can be trusted with the lives of others. As a very extroverted homeschooler, it was the perfect job for me. I was challenged, I worked with kids and seniors, and I made friends who were also colleagues.

But the YMCA is also where I felt left out for the first time. Although these kids were responsible, they weren't Christian, so they did party at times. Sometimes I got invited to these parties. I'd politely turn down the invitation and then go home while I knew all my friends were off having a great time without me. And that was hard for me.

No matter how frustrated I was that I always missed out, I never went to a single party in high school. And it wasn't even because my parents told me I couldn't go. I just didn't want to— because no matter how sad I was that I wasn't having fun with my friends, I never felt that giving up what I had with my family and with God was worth it. Instead of seeing it as "They get to have all this fun, and I don't get to have any," my view was that I had simply chosen a different life. And my life was full of fun, albeit very different fun.

A huge part of that was that my family was a fun family. We had our own unique family culture that made me feel that, although I didn't have what my coworkers had, I had something better. So the partying wasn't a temptation. Instead, we went on camping trips and vacations together. We went out for dessert to celebrate when someone succeeded. My dad would even play *Rock Band* with us on our Wii. But the main thing above all was that my parents were my friends. I truly wanted to spend time with them. Having them as friends meant that I had an alternate way of life that was also a lot of fun while still living in a way that pleased God.

Often when parents try to be friends with their kids, though, it goes terribly wrong. I had a friend when I was fourteen whose mom wanted to be the "cool mom." In an attempt to connect with her daughter, she tried to get in on the youth group's gossip and giggle about it as if she were one of the girls. I'd sit down for lunch with Naomi, and her mom would pop in with a "Hey, girlfriends! What's the latest?" And then she'd giggle and chat at us until we spilled. She would go through her daughter's closet and pull out tops and ask, "Do you think this would fit me? Isn't it so cute we have the same style!"

It was weird seeing an adult woman acting like a fourteen-year-old girl. And it was always awkward and forced. She was a nice lady and a very responsible adult. But her daughter did not respect her, and I found it uncomfortable.

The problem is that when parents try to be friends with their kids, often it becomes a situation similar to Naomi's. In every other part of her life, Naomi's mom was a respected professional woman with her own business. She was not flighty in the least. But when trying to be friends with her daughter, Naomi's mother changed so that her daughter would want to be friends with her too. And it backfired.

My parents never tried to change to fit in with us or with our friends. They were simply themselves, take it or leave it. We didn't gossip about who liked whom in the youth group, and we didn't giggle in blanket forts late at night like I did with my friends who were my age. That would be ridiculous—they were adults. Instead we went on walks together, talked while making dinner, and laughed at Dad while he tried to play *Rock Band*. We were friends, and my parents expected us to like them for who they were, not as some cool-parent version of themselves.

When I talked to other kids who didn't rebel, I found the same thing: kids who didn't rebel were friends with their parents.

They spent time together, they knew their parents' hopes and dreams, and they had their own traditions. For all of us, our families were where we really felt that we belonged.

HONESTY: PARENTS ADMITTING THEY AREN'T PERFECT

One of my most potent memories about my dad's work from when I was a kid was that it was stressful. My dad is a pediatrician, and for a while he was one of only two pediatricians in an area with more than 120,000 people. He was on call almost all the time, and when he wasn't, he was still exhausted from being on call. Sometimes he had to make hard choices, and sometimes the kid didn't pull through. Every day he dealt with families going through the worst times of their lives, and when he came home he was often completely drained.

As a result, although I would say about 90 percent of the time my family was happy and engaged with each other, there was that small percentage where we had a slightly detached, stressed daddy. And it wasn't predictable—it wasn't every time he was on call, for instance. And that lack of predictability can be hard on a little kid.

My parents were very open about Daddy's stress at work. When Daddy had a particularly tough day, Mom would pull us aside and tell us to play quietly in our rooms for a little bit or to be extra nice to Daddy because he'd had to give some parents very bad news that day. Sometimes when he came home after an extra-bad day at work, he would lose his temper and yell at us if we hadn't done our chores or if we bickered a little bit— something that normally would only get a firm warning. But whenever he lost his temper, he would cool off and then come back and talk to us about it instead of letting it fester. Because we talked about work stress so much, it didn't worry me much at all—and I'm a very high-strung person. I never worried that Daddy would be anything other than all right, because we talked about everything—it wasn't a scary, unknown monster but a problem that my family presented as resolvable and spoke to us about from a young age.

Imagine being thrown into the middle of a dance, not knowing any of the steps. Wouldn't you want nothing more than to just get out of there? I know I would. But what if you had all the steps already memorized? It's a lot less scary when you know what's coming. Being honest with kids is like giving them the steps to the dance. Because my parents told me what was worrying them, I knew what I was facing. And I knew that my parents were taking care of it. So I didn't feel like I was drowning in uncertainty.

A surprising finding from my interviews was that kids who didn't rebel had parents who were willing to admit their flaws.

- "My dad was always the first to admit he was wrong. When he yelled at us or said something he didn't mean, he'd go outside and take a walk to cool off; then he'd come back and apologize and ask for forgiveness for what he had said."
- "My parents were both very busy people. So when they

had a rough day, they'd sometimes lose their tempers. They would explain that they had been very stressed from work and then ask for forgiveness for letting that stress get the better of them. They gave reasons but never rationalized what they had done, so I knew they were really sorry."

Often when parents are dealing with something difficult, such as work stress, they feel as though they should shelter their children from it. However, in the families where teens didn't rebel, they often knew pretty much everything that was going on, and they fared better for it. Children are very perceptive, and teens are even more perceptive than little kids—we can tell when there's something wrong, and it's much scarier when we don't know what we're facing.

Remember Courtney from the last chapter? Her family, although they chatted all the time, never opened up about what was important. Instead of sitting down and discussing the mental-health issues in their family, the family never talked about it because her mom wasn't willing to admit she didn't have it under control. So when Courtney grew into a teenager, she didn't have a true relationship with her mom. And she looked for that relationship elsewhere.

Often parents focus so much on creating the perfect family that they forget the basics of any relationship: just be friends with each other. And being friends means you need to open up and admit when you are wrong.

But do openness and honesty between parents and children really work in cases where the issues are big? How about with marriage issues? Should parents be open with their children about those? According to Morgan, talking to your kids about marriage problems can make the situation much easier for them.

Morgan's father had an affair when Morgan was ten, and it tore apart her family. He moved to a house down the street. But although they all saw each other frequently, tensions were high and Morgan's life changed drastically. However, even through the midst of it, Morgan was able to talk openly with her mom about what was going on and how it was affecting her. "I wasn't as comfortable talking about it with Dad at the time," Morgan told me, "but I talked about it a lot with Mom. My parents both openly acknowledged that what Dad had done was wrong, and my dad did apologize to me, and later we were able to have some honest conversations about how it affected me too." Later her parents reconciled, and their openness about their struggles helped Morgan process what was happening.

Talking about it didn't make everything better—that's not what I'm suggesting. Morgan wasn't magically unaffected by her parents' separation, and I wasn't perfectly fine even though I knew why Daddy was stressed. What talking to kids *does* do, though, is show the child, "Hey, this is happening. There's no escaping it. But we're in this together and we've got each other's back."

True relationships require honesty. Without honesty in a relationship there is no way to get to know the person. If you're friends with someone but he or she never wants to disclose anything, it doesn't seem like a real friendship, does it? It's the same way with children. Yes, there are boundaries. Morgan's family didn't tell their children the details of the affair. But they were honest about it. When we were younger, my family didn't go into detail about what had happened to Dad at work because they didn't want to put his stress on our shoulders. But age-appropriate disclosure is the first step to that closeness all of us felt with our parents.

Now, honesty isn't just important with the big, serious issues. It's also important to be able to acknowledge flaws. This year my family went on a cruise together. It was the first vacation we had gone on since I got married, so it was Connor's initiation into the Gregoire family vacation tradition: watch my mother go absolutely nuts while trying to get ready to go out the door.

My mom isn't exactly Martha Stewart. She keeps a lovely home and is a clean person, but we're not Monica-from-*Friends* clean. When we leave for vacations, though, that all changes. Suddenly, although they haven't bothered her at all since the last vacation, the baseboards are despicably dirty. And how can she be expected to get on a plane when the baseboards are dusty back home?

Needless to say, having to leave to catch a plane in an hour with your mom screaming at you about the baseboards is not a pleasant experience. But it's one that we've come to accept as reality because it happens before every vacation. Every. Single. One. "I just can't stand the stress of coming home to a messy house!"

So when Connor was preparing for his first Gregoire vacation, we all warned him: "Get ready to clean some baseboards!" It's become the family joke. And Mom laughs too.

If they are to have a real relationship with their parents, kids need to be allowed to be honest about the situation. You can't be friends with someone who doesn't admit when he or she is wrong or can't laugh at his or her flaws.

When a family is honest, it lets the children understand where they fit in the situation. That's why honesty about flaws and struggles is what makes children go from simply being part of a family to truly belonging in it. In contrast, when these things aren't talked about, it makes it harder for the children to feel that they truly belong. How can you belong somewhere you can't speak your mind?

Being honest with children gives them certainty about the present. Mom and Dad have taken away the fear that comes with the unknown. So there isn't the need to escape the present, even if the present is hard. It's the difference between an eleven-year-old who dresses and acts like a sixteen-year-old because she's desperate to escape the present and an eleven-year-old who is perfectly content with just being eleven. Even something simple, like letting your kids joke about your psychopathological stress response to travel, can make all the difference.

BUILDING A FRIENDSHIP: JUST HANGING OUT

Obviously, just telling your kids all your flaws and letting them acknowledge when you've done things wrong isn't enough to create that sense of belonging. As with any relationship, building a friendship requires spending enormous amounts of time together.

Now, often when we think of spending time with family, we immediately jump to having dinner together, taking vacations, and having game nights. Those things are very important and a lot of fun, but they can also seem forced and awkward if there is no relationship *other* than these activities.

True friends aren't only there for game nights or vacations—they're the people we spend our downtime with. Doing nothing together is how you truly get to know someone and how he or she becomes a natural part of your life. It's the same with children, and Rachel and Jacob's story shows us why.

If there is one thing that is clear about Rachel and Jacob's family, it's that they are very close. Despite living in different cities, the siblings and their parents visit each other frequently, and they all FaceTime on a regular basis, making sure everyone is caught up on what's going on in everyone's lives.

"The main thing that made our family so close," Rachel explained, "is that we spent a whole lot of time together." They did all the typical things that you're supposed to do to have a close family, like eat dinner together and have game nights, but they took it one step further. "Instead of just eating dinner together, we were expected to eat breakfast and lunch with whoever was home. If we were doing homework or goofing off on our laptops or phones, we did it in the living room or kitchen, all together. It was never explicitly said that we always had to spend time together, but our parents would encourage us to make that choice in the moment. They would say, 'Hey, Jacob, if you're doing your homework, why not do it at the table with the rest of us?' So it just became natural to do things together, even if we weren't really doing anything in particular." By the time Rachel and Jacob were teenagers, this had been the routine for so long that it didn't seem like a big deal to spend so much time together—it was just a natural part of their lives.

Their family also had more intense periods of family time whenever they went on vacation. "Vacations were really important to us as a family," Jacob explained. "We went to Florida for a week or two in the winter and to the cottage for a week or two in the summer. When we went away, it was strictly family time. We didn't have our phones or our computers, and we didn't bring a bunch of friends. We would go by ourselves, with our cousins, or with this one family that we went to Florida with every year. But we always went as a family with another family—not a bunch of kids bringing friends." Jacob's brow furrowed. "I never really understand why some families bring friends on vacation—some of my friends, when they went away, were allowed to bring whoever they chose. But if all the kids have a friend along, you never actually see your family the whole time!"

Rachel shrugged. "To us, it just never made any sense."

Having a natural routine of spending time with family coupled with more intense family time together on vacations profoundly impacted both Rachel's and Jacob's view of their parents. "Since we saw our parents so much, we didn't only see them when they were mad and yelling at us," Rachel said, laughing. "I know a lot of my friends really only talked to their parents when they were in trouble. But because we saw our parents in so many different contexts, the way we interacted really changed."

"It sounds silly," Jacob added, "but we saw our parents as

people more than we did as just parents. We knew that what we said to our parents could hurt them as much as the same words could hurt us. I don't think that many teens understand that about parents—that how you act is going to really affect them."

Our family was huge on spending time together too. We homeschooled, so it was easier for us than for most, but looking back on my childhood and even teenage years, it's very hard to think of times when I *wasn't* with my mom or my dad. We were always showing each other funny jokes we found online, knitting while we watched Netflix, or simply hanging out in the living room, even if we weren't actually doing anything together.

A study by Dr. Shira Offer found that on average, teens spend about twenty hours a week with their parents.[1] In her study she also examined the types of activities teens did with parents and how that impacted the quality of their relationship with their parents. What she found was that leisure time had the most positive impact on their relationship, whereas things like shuttling children back and forth from activities or doing chores together made teens less engaged in the relationship.[2] Specifically, spending leisure time together was related to increases in teenagers' emotional well-being[3]—just doing nothing together helps kids thrive. And that is because spending so much time together, even when you're doing nothing, shows kids that you like being around them. There isn't pressure to perform or to earn affection—they simply have it.

Letting kids speak truth about the situation helps them accept the present and be comfortable with where they are.

Spending time together shows children they are free to be themselves. It's the third step that brings it all together.

CREATING A FAMILY CULTURE: GIVING THEM SOMETHING BETTER

Everyone who meets Joanna's family immediately wants to become a part of it. And neither Joanna nor her three other siblings rebelled—largely because, I think, of their family culture.

My favorite story that epitomizes the feel of this family is the story of the yellow pants. One day Joanna was out shopping with her father when they found the most hideous yellow pants you could possibly imagine. They were loud, they were bright, and they looked as if they belonged on Ronald McDonald. They practically glowed in the dark. So Joanna dared her dad to buy them. When she unveiled them in front of the family, everyone burst out laughing.

Joanna begged her dad to wear them to the next Bible Quizzing Tournament she and her siblings were competing in, and he said, "Why not?" He showed up, and they were a hit. And he's worn them to every winter quizzing tournament in the past ten years. He doesn't mind kids laughing at him; he wants to be part of the fun.

"I loved being a part of my family," Joanna explained. "We had a real Connelly family culture. There were a lot of things that were our trademark. We played cards with Dad after dinner, we skied, and had really silly traditions at Christmas." When I asked her what some of these traditions were, she laughed and continued, "Well, the silliest part is that we have an improv Christmas pageant every year with the family. We choose a different perspective of the Christmas story, and it always ends up with everyone crying, they are laughing so hard. Last year my husband ended up in my grandmother's mink coat with a horrible Russian accent. You just never know what's going to happen."

Joanna's family understood that to raise kids who won't rebel, you have to give them an alternative to rebelling. Just saying, "Don't rebel" and then not giving them anything else can lead to children feeling as though they are missing out without getting anything in return. The way Joanna's family circumvented that was through creating this family culture where they did lots of fun things. The biggest one, according to Joanna, was Bible Quizzing.

"Quizzing was our life," Joanna explained. "Everyone did it—Mom and Dad coached at all our meets, and it was so fun to have a family thing everyone did together." Their family revolved around quizzing—in a way it became their family identity. *What do the Connellys do? The Connellys quiz.*

"It helped that we are naturally a competitive family," Joanna remarked, "so we all wanted to do the best we could. On long car rides we listened to tapes of the chapters we were memorizing, we quizzed each other on our verses, and Mom and Dad would help us train for meets. But my parents were always clear that we didn't only do it to win—we quizzed because it was a fun thing to do, it was a great way to learn the Bible, and it was an amazing opportunity to make tons of friends who were also Christians."

Having family activities fostered friendships between

Joanna, her siblings, and her parents. Joanna's parents strengthened this by getting to know each child individually. "I remember
one time," Joanna told me, "when Mom was driving my brother,
Johnny, and me back from school, and my brother was telling
Mom all about his kickball game that day at recess. It was so
boring. And in that moment I thought, *Mom probably doesn't
actually find this interesting, either, but she's listening because she
wants to learn about what's important to Johnny.* That was a huge
revelation for me—that Mom might not find everything about
us all that interesting, but she wanted to get to know us anyway."

Because Joanna's parents knew each of their children so
well, they were able to have fun together without anyone feeling
left out. "My dad loved to reward us for our successes," Joanna
explained, "and he always made it into a game. My youngest
sister could hang off the molding on the doorframe using only
her toes, so we'd all gather around; Dad would stand under her,
ready to catch her; and we'd count to see how long she could stay
up." Joanna smiled. "It was all sorts of things like that. My game
was that if I could stump Dad with one of the questions I had to
answer at school, I got a quarter. I loved it, and it was particularly
fun when I found a whole subject that he wasn't very good at."

An important aspect to celebrating the uniqueness of each
child was that no one had to compete at something that wasn't
his or her gifting. Joanna never had to hang upside down from
the doorframe, because that definitely would have sent someone
to the emergency room. Everyone was celebrated for who they
were—they each belonged individually, even though they were
so different from one another.

Having a strong friendship with her parents gave Joanna and her siblings an alternative to rebelling. They were celebrated for their uniqueness, were part of a fun family, and had a place where they always fit in—and where they *wanted* to fit in. "A great deal of why we didn't rebel is because of our family culture." Joanna shrugged. "We were different, and it was okay. We had somewhere else to belong."

OFFERING SOMETHING BETTER

When I was invited to parties with my friends from work, I said no. It was frustrating that I didn't get to spend as much time with them because I refused to have anything to do with drinking in high school, but it was never a hard decision. I had something better than parties—I had a family who really liked me.

But that's often not the case in many families. Most families, even if the parents do really *like* their kids, don't have that friendship. So parents teach their children, "You shouldn't do these things," but don't offer the kids anything to fill that void. There isn't a family they really belong to that takes the place of the peer approval you find at parties. The children feel as though they're missing something. And they look for it in the wrong places. Listen to what some of my interviewees said about why they rebelled:

- "I got in with the bad crowd because they had my back and believed in me. My parents didn't."

- "Not doing bad stuff like having sex and drinking alcohol seemed to be too hard without anything in return. So I gave in."
- "I thought that I was the problem and that my family would be better off if I wasn't there. So I left."

None of these kids had a family like Joanna, Jacob and Rachel, Morgan, or I did. They didn't have that friendship, that place to belong, so being good wasn't worth it. And they looked for that belonging somewhere else.

Raising kids who don't rebel means raising kids who are going to be different. We're not going to fit in most places. We're going to miss out on some typical high school rites of passage (even though it's for the better). But we who don't rebel have something that makes missing out on those things seem insignificant: we have somewhere else we truly belong.

6

DISCIPLINE

KEEPING THE END GOAL IN MIND

When I was four I committed my first crime. My mom and I were in a craft store, picking up some supplies. As I wandered up and down the aisles of pipe cleaners and pom-poms, I spotted something: tiny, miniature stuffed bears and rabbits.

I had to have them.

It was March and we lived in Canada, which means that I was wearing my winter parka. Those coats have *big* pockets. I grabbed the little animals and stuffed my pockets full while my mom paid for her items. We walked out to the car, I got buckled in, and we were on our way.

I was happily humming "Jesus Loves Me" when we pulled into the driveway. Mom unbuckled me, picked me up, and felt the incriminating lumps. "Becca," she asked, "what's in your pockets?"

Smiling, excited to show my mommy my new toys, I emptied

my pockets of what must have been thirty little toy bears and rab-bits. "Look!" I told her. "I'm going to show them to the cousins!"

My mom closed her eyes, took a deep breath, and said, "Becca, you can't just take things—that is stealing. And stealing is wrong. We need to take the little bears and bunnies back."

As a four-year-old, I hadn't even considered that it might be wrong to take the pretty little bunnies and the tiny little ted-dies. I was mortified and definitely did not like the idea of taking them back to the store. But Mom would not be swayed. We drove all the way back, she marched me back to the lady behind the counter, and she made me explain what I had done. I gave a sniv-eling apology while the store manager tried not to laugh at the quivering little thief standing in front of her. I handed over the contraband, asked for forgiveness, and then we went back home. I never stole again.

When I look back on how my parents disciplined me, I remember a lot of these consequence-based punishments from when I was a kid. But I don't remember many from when I was a teen. So I asked other people who didn't rebel about how they were disciplined when they were teens, and they said the same thing: they couldn't remember.

- "I don't remember a single time I was actually punished for anything after age nine or so. I got chastised when I made a bad decision, but it was always more of a conversation about what I did wrong instead of having these huge con-sequences, like being grounded for a month or something."
- "When I did something wrong in high school, my parents

always surprised me. I expected them to lay down the law and crack down on me to make sure my behavior stopped, but they didn't. Instead, they'd give me a big hug, and we'd talk about why it was wrong. Then we'd make a plan together so that they could keep me accountable. But I was never really punished."

- "I don't remember ever really being punished, like being grounded or anything, in high school. If I made a mistake, we'd talk about it, but then they trusted I wouldn't purposefully do it again, so they didn't need to punish."

Those who did rebel, on the other hand, *were* disciplined as teenagers. But that's only logical—of course they would be disciplined if they were rebelling. Maybe the difference, then, started much further back, in childhood. Was there some way that discipline earlier in our lives influenced whether or not we rebelled?

DISCIPLINE IN THE EARLY YEARS

Usually when we hear *discipline* and *children*, we immediately think *spanking*. I was never spanked, though, and Katie was only spanked once. It was when she was around four and had been refusing to listen to Mom, so she was sent to her room to cool off. She was having none of it. So my mom said, "Katie, you go to your room or—"

"Or what?" Katie demanded.

"Or . . . I'll give you a spanking."

This was a big deal in my house. As I said, spanking just didn't happen.

Katie became quiet. She maintained eye contact for a few seconds before asking, "How many spanks?"

"Ten," my mom replied, trying to give her a number big enough that she'd go to her room and stop making a fuss.

Katie thought again. After a long pause she nodded once, crossed her arms, and said, "I'll take the spanks." And my mom, not wanting to fail to follow through, had to spank her ten times.

One difference I found in my interviews was that the frequency of spanking seemed to differ between families with kids who did rebel and who didn't. The majority of kids who rebelled told me they were spanked regularly as kids, even if it wasn't the primary form of discipline in the house. They had similar answers, which were generally along the lines of "I was definitely spanked as a kid, but I'm not sure it actually did much."

In contrast, kids who didn't rebel tended to be spanked less, or only for very specific reasons. Most kids who didn't rebel had stories similar to Parker's.

"I wasn't spanked all that often," Parker told me. "But I remember one time very clearly. I was about two or three at the time, and I decided to play hide-and-seek with Mom and Dad. But I didn't tell them I wanted to play—I just hid." Parker laughed. "And I hid *really* well. I was tiny, and I curled up in the back corner of a closet, knees to my chest. And I stayed there for two or three hours. My parents were freaking out. They looked everywhere and couldn't find me. They called my name, and I didn't answer because I was so proud of how well I had hidden. After about an hour and a half, my parents started running up and down the street, knocking on all our neighbors' doors, asking if they had seen me. My dad found me just as my mom was about to call the police."

Parker laughed. "I got a spanking after that. But I really wasn't spanked very often, and only ever as a last resort."

Similar to Parker, most kids who didn't rebel were spanked rarely.

- Lily's parents only spanked when she lied.
- Samantha's mom only spanked when Samantha was out of control and her mom needed to get her attention or she might hurt herself.
- Amelia's parents only spanked after she had gotten a warning, they'd had a discussion about why the behavior was wrong, and she'd still done it.

However, I still didn't think I'd found enough information to posit any themes among kids who did and didn't rebel when it came to spanking. So I turned to an expert in the field, Dr. Elisa Romano, a clinical psychologist specializing in child maltreatment and family psychology. I e-mailed her, asking if we could meet and discuss this, and two weeks later we were chatting in her office.

"When it comes to the effects of spanking," Dr. Romano explained, "Gershoff's meta-analysis with over 120,000 participants is the place to look. Gershoff is the world's foremost researcher on the issue, and this particular study is amazing because it analyzed data from seventy-five studies, so Gershoff's results are really a summary of all the applicable literature. What she found was that spanking does not have any positive outcomes. There was only one neutral outcome, which was immediate compliance. But there were thirteen other outcomes that were all negative. These included increased aggression, a less close parent-child relationship, and an increased risk for mental-health issues during childhood."[1]

"So," I asked, "if spanking can be so bad, why do parents continue spanking their children?"

"Parents are not out to do their children harm," Dr. Romano was quick to say. "They spank because they see that spanking works. If they spank, right away the child stops the behavior. That is very powerful for parents, and seeing it work is enough to make them spank again in the future. But even if spanking stops the behavior right now, it doesn't help the child long term.

"People often assume there can't be anything wrong with spanking," Dr. Romano continued, "because they turned out just fine. But that is not an accurate interpretation of the research. Research shows that experiencing spanking puts you at risk—you have a higher likelihood of having these negative effects than someone who wasn't spanked. But simply being at risk does not guarantee that you *will* have these outcomes. The argument is similar to someone saying, 'My mom drank alcohol when she was pregnant with me, and I'm fine, so it's okay that I drink alcohol while I'm pregnant.' None of us would agree with that statement, but it's the same with spanking. Of course many people who were spanked grew up fine. But why should a child be hit when we know of alternatives to spanking that are much more effective? Why inflict pain when you don't have to?"[2]

Wow. That seems pretty heavy. After years of meticulous research, we can safely say that spanking does not tend to produce positive effects. But why is that? Shiloh's story might help shed light on the matter.

FEARING THE CONSEQUENCE WITHOUT LEARNING RESPECT

As with the rules in chapter 2, Shiloh's parents based their discipline around religion. "My parents were very strong believers in the 'Spare the rod, spoil the child' Christian mentality," Shiloh explained. "They spanked us frequently, but they said that they did it in love and because the Bible told them to. I don't think they ever explored any alternatives." Shiloh frowned. "I also find it somewhat disturbing that they spanked me until I was twelve. It seemed normal at the time, but it's unsettling looking back now that I'm older."

One of the issues that Shiloh found with spanking was that it didn't teach her or her siblings any real lessons. "Spanking never made me feel sorry for what I had done," Shiloh explained. "We just took the punishment, pretended to be remorseful, and then just moved on. It really didn't mold our character.

"For my brothers, especially," Shiloh continued, "spanking only worked until we were too big for our parents to be able to physically dominate us. When they got older, my brothers just kept misbehaving because they weren't afraid anymore of getting spanked. So although it worked to keep us from being bad when we were younger, it really didn't seem to produce any real respect in the long term."

But simply being ineffective wasn't the only issue with spanking in Shiloh's house. "Unfortunately," Shiloh told me, "I do have vivid memories of one time my parents were spanking my brother and it escalated into a physical altercation. Seeing that really affected, if not traumatized, my brothers and me psychologically and emotionally." Shiloh shook her head. "It still makes my stomach turn to remember what happened. Although I do remind myself that my parents were only doing what they had been taught by Christian parenting curriculums back then. They truly never meant to cause any harm." Shiloh shrugged. "They just didn't know what else to do."

"HE WHO SPARES THE ROD . . ."

The verse that is most often quoted to support spanking in families like Shiloh's is Proverbs 13:24: "He who spares the rod hates his son, / but he who loves him is diligent to discipline him" (RSV). It seems straightforward—not spanking kids is bad for kids, and good parents spank. But after hearing Shiloh's story, coupled with the research, I wanted to make sure we had it right. So I turned to Samuel Martin, a Christian theologian known for his in-depth theological analyses of biblical texts that are used to promote spanking.

"In your expert opinion as a theologian," I asked Mr. Martin, "does the Bible support using spanking for discipline?"

"The short answer is no," he replied, "but it's more complicated than that. Because the verses *do* advocate corporal punishment. The problem is in our interpretation of the original text."

I was glad he acknowledged how complicated an issue this is. "So," I asked, "where are our mistakes?"

"First," Mr. Martin began, "there is a fundamental misunderstanding of the age of the son in these passages. Virtually every time someone advocates spanking, he or she says that the Bible teaches to spank *children*."

Well, sure. But isn't that what the passage says?

Not so fast. In three verses that are commonly used in the spanking debate—and the only three that talk about using a rod—the Hebrew word for "son" that is used is *na'ar*. This word refers to a young man in young adulthood or in his teenage years. "This is significant," Mr. Martin said, both in our interview as well as in his book. "Based on this evidence, it is safe to say that all these texts in the book of Proverbs have no application to anyone less than about ten to twelve years of age.[3]

"Also," Mr. Martin explained, "the sociocultural environment of the time was so incredibly different from our own. The society was based on family honor. At the time that this was written, corporal punishment for young men was important because if they did something wrong, what was waiting for them outside the house was so much worse. If they didn't change, they were going to be beaten or, in some cases, executed. Capital punishment had many laws governing its use, but boys as young as thirteen could face grave consequences if they were legally subject to biblical law and had broken one of the binding laws of the time.

"Taking these issues into account, it is not appropriate to read the Bible and apply it literally in our individual contexts," Mr. Martin said. "There really is no biblical basis for spanking children in today's society."

IF NOT SPANKING, THEN WHAT?

After hearing Shiloh's story, coupled with the research and the theological study that Samuel had done, the argument against spanking made a lot of sense.

But I wasn't content with just saying spanking was bad and then moving on. If research has shown that spanking as a main form of discipline isn't effective, then how *do* parents discipline?

I started asking kids who didn't rebel to find out. And the first person I talked to was Dylan.

BALANCING CONTROL AND WARMTH

Dylan was the youngest of his family, with one older sister and, like many of us who didn't rebel, he doesn't remember being disciplined regularly as a teenager. But that doesn't mean he was *never* disciplined.

"I was a handful when I was a kid," Dylan said with a chuckle, "but my parents didn't really need to discipline me very often when I hit the teenage years because they put in a lot of work when I was younger. I think because they started teaching us how to behave so early, it made it easier for them when we were older." Dylan shrugged. "By the time I was a preteen, my parents had pretty much taught me how not to be a brat."

"So how did your parents discipline you, then?" I asked.

"Well, they had a variety of methods," Dylan explained. "Some worked; some didn't. One of the biggest flops was when my mom tried to use hot peppers to discipline. She'd make us eat one whenever we said a bad word, but after two or three times we started to really like them. We'd open our mouths like little birds waiting to be fed. So that one backfired.

"For the most part, though, my parents mainly used consequences to help coach us, in a sense, to become better people," Dylan answered. "They did spank me at times, when I was very young, but it was only if nothing else worked first. And they were always sad when they had to spank us—we knew that they didn't want to, so it was always their last resort, and it really wasn't that often. In general, the punishments they gave us were consequence based so they could help teach us that our actions have consequences. If I told my mom the food was gross, for instance, before I even tried it, I wouldn't be allowed to have dessert, because I had been rude about the food that Mom had worked hard on. My parents would explain that I had been rude and hurt her feelings, and so I didn't get dessert, because dessert was a luxury.

"We always openly talked about the reasons like that too— they explained why they didn't want us behaving certain ways, and we had many talks about what it meant to be a good person and how our actions were or were not helping us become one."

However, Dylan's family wasn't *only* focused on discipline. Dylan's parents also put a great deal of effort in showing their kids how much they cared about them.

"Our parents were also really fun," Dylan said. "It wasn't that my parents were drill sergeants or anything—they were also really enjoyable people. My dad used to let me ski behind his four-wheeler when it snowed, and we would all toss around the football in the summer. We also used to have a ton of movie and game nights after dinner when I was a kid." Dylan smiled. "It definitely wasn't only strict discipline—it was a good balance. They were in charge, but they were also a ton of fun.

"By the time I got to high school," Dylan told me, "I knew where I fit. Yes, I had a lot of boundaries, and I knew there were things that I shouldn't do, but they made sense to me because my parents had explained it so many times. Also, it didn't seem unfair. I liked my parents, I knew they liked me, and their discipline didn't crush all the fun—just the fun that really wasn't beneficial for me."

Dylan's family is the perfect example of the authoritative parenting style we talked about in the rules chapter. Providing children with structure (being a parent) while also showing them a lot of warmth (being a friend) helps children thrive.

SEEING DIFFERENCES BETWEEN MISBEHAVIOR AND BEING A KID

We're talking a lot about warmth when it comes to discipline, but normally we don't think about warmth and discipline in the same sentence. After all, discipline needs to be about being firm when you're disappointed, while warmth is about love when you're happy, right? But maybe one of the reasons that discipline doesn't work is because parents forget the importance of warmth in their quest to make kids obey. Let me explain with a story.

When I was about sixteen, our family visited an aquarium. I love everything to do with marine biology, so I was in paradise. But one display was difficult to enjoy because a four-year-old boy was yelling and singing at the top of his lungs, running back and forth, and just generally being a nuisance. And his parents would threaten him with time-outs or that they would leave if he didn't stop . . . and then go right back to their conversation.

I eventually got fed up. So I started talking to the kid. "Hey, buddy," I said. "Do you see that fish right there?" He nodded. "It's called a boxfish. Can you tell me why?"

"'Cause it's shaped like a box!" he said.

"That's right! Let's try to find some more boxfish! How many do you think there are?"

"One . . . two . . . three . . ."

And the conversation continued. The kid went from running around, out of control, to being an absolute delight. He wasn't a bad kid—he was just really bored.

I can only remember one time from when I was a kid that I was a real brat in public. I'm sure there were more, but only one from my older childhood really stands out. Last minute, my mom had brought six-year-old Katie and eight-year-old me with her to a pottery store so she could order my nana a custom piece for Christmas. My mom looked through the entire inventory and was seated, designing a teapot that Katie and I could not have cared less about. And the store had an amazing staircase. So Katie and I started playing. We ran up and down the stairs, yelling and having fun. About five minutes into our playing, my mom marched into the room, dragged us out the door, and buckled us into our car seats. We knew we were in trouble.

"What were you thinking?" she yelled, "You do not act like that in a store with delicate art. You could have broken something, and that was very wrong and very rude."

But all I remembered was being bored. Katie and I had been sitting quietly for half an hour before we got up and started playing. And that's a long time for a little kid. Katie and I came on these kinds of errands with Mom all the time, but this was the first time we had gotten into trouble. And the reason was that all the other times, we had been prepared. I remember Mom used to chat with us in the morning saying things like, "We're going to the dentist today, so we'll be in the waiting room for a while. What would you like to bring to do while you're in the waiting room?" And we would choose what schoolwork to bring or a book to read or maybe a journal to write in. We always had something to do to keep us occupied.

This time was different. We had driven to the store last minute, without preparing anything for us to do. My mom had thought it would be a quick five-minute errand and didn't realize how long a process it was going to be. So although Katie and I were definitely wrong for running around in a pottery store, it didn't mean we had been bad kids. And after she calmed down, my mom saw that too. On the way home we all talked about things we could do instead of being loud and rowdy when we got bored in public.

Instead of punishing boredom, it's very easy to just fix the problem behind the behavior in these kinds of situations. I think that may be why I was so frustrated with the parents at the aquarium—they were yelling at their little boy when he was just bored. So I followed my parents' example and tried to take away the boredom. And immediately the behavior changed.

This goes hand in hand with the importance of the authoritative parenting we saw in Dylan's family, according to Dr. Romano. If you're parenting in a way that involves explaining consequences and hearing your child's perspective on the matter, you're going to be better equipped to anticipate problems before they even happen, like how my parents would encourage us to choose an activity to prepare for when we were going somewhere boring.

While parents shouldn't punish boredom, says Dr. Romano, they should also look out for developmental stages and temperament. It's the difference between seeing a two-year-old throwing food as being bad or as simply being a two-year-old. "Many children, when they misbehave, aren't being defiant or oppositional," Dr. Romano explained, "but are reacting normally to the situation considering their age or their temperament."[4] Two-year-olds are just going to throw things. Children who are very shy or who have difficult temperaments are going to find new situations harder than children with more easygoing temperaments. By knowing these things about their children, parents can actually prevent misbehavior as my mom did by bringing us books or schoolwork when we had to run errands.

Even the most perfectly prepared parents, though, are

eventually going to run smack into some behavior that just isn't acceptable. What do they do then?

SEEING MISBEHAVIOR AS A CHANCE FOR GROWTH

I have always had problems with emotional regulation. I just never seemed to quite get the hang of the whole emotional-control thing. I would get overwhelmed and burst into tears or throw a mini fit when I was in kindergarten, and I often had a very hard time even recognizing what I was feeling. I couldn't always tell if I was extremely happy or extremely angry. I was just overwhelmed.

The majority of the times I misbehaved as a kid were directly related to emotional issues. I would get angry with Katie and yell at her, or I would get extremely sad and snap at Mom. And since most of my misbehavior revolved around my emotions, most of my discipline did too.

But I don't remember being *punished* for having emotional outbursts, even though I was disciplined. I wasn't spanked for not being able to handle my emotions, didn't have dessert taken away. Instead, my parents followed three steps.

First, they would talk to me about why I had acted out. If I did something like hitting Katie, they knew it wasn't because I was a violent person. It was because I had gotten too angry and didn't know how to control it. Second, they would use the situation as an opportunity to teach me about right and wrong. They would explain why the behavior wasn't right and why I shouldn't do it again. Third, they would give me alternatives for my behavior. We would talk about noticing when I was getting emotional, recognizing what I was feeling, and brainstorming ways to calm down, such as going to my room for alone time. The closest it came to punishment was when my parents had to force me to have alone time. But even then, they always explained that alone time was a good way to calm down and that it wasn't a punishment, just a way to help me get control back. Then I would apologize to whomever I hurt or take care of the damage done, and I would be back to playing.

By using my outbursts as a chance to help teach me emotional-regulation skills, my parents gave me a chance to grow that I simply would not have gotten if I had just been punished instead of coached through my emotions; this coaching helped deal with the underlying issue behind my misbehavior instead of just dealing with the symptom.

This was the most effective discipline method my parents used when I was a teenager as well. In fact, the only time my relationship with my parents was less than great was when they didn't use this method. When I was sixteen, I had my heart broken for the first time and I wasn't able to handle it. I wasn't prepared, and all the issues I had with emotional control didn't help much either.

My parents knew I was sad, but when I didn't get better after a month or two, they started getting irritated—and for good reason. I was really annoying. I moped all the time, I was extremely angry, I lost all motivation, and I was determined to make sure everyone was as miserable as I was so they'd just understand.

We got into screaming matches multiple times a week—my parents were at a loss, my sister was walking on eggshells, and I was a mess. My parents started to try to punish me for my emotional outbursts, and that only seemed to make it worse.

What none of us realized was that I was depressed. Not just moody, but legitimately depressed.

The turning point came during one of our biggest fights, almost four months into my depression. My mom was yelling because of how frustrated she was that I couldn't sit down and get through one unit of psychology—what I was hoping to do for the rest of my life. My dad was angry because I was making everyone else miserable because of how abysmal my attitude had been lately. And I lost it. I started screaming at them.

"I don't care! I don't care about any of it! I just want you to see how much I'm hurting and how much I don't know how to stop it."

My parents stopped, went quiet, and we all just sat together for what must have been two hours of tears and prayer. My parents talked to me about depression, and we worked on some ways to challenge the negative thoughts I was having by teaching me to compare what I was feeling to what God's Word had to say. They didn't allow me to continue having my outbursts, but they stopped punishing me for being depressed. It wasn't fixed overnight, and I didn't fully recover for another four years after that. But having my parents understand that I wasn't trying to misbehave was the saving grace for our relationship and the first step toward my recovery.

But just talking about it doesn't work for everything. What do you do when kids have a real behavior issue that needs to be resolved?

THE POWER OF NATURAL CONSEQUENCES

When Tommy was three, he despised getting dressed. Every morning was a battle, and it didn't matter how often he was told he had to get out of his pajamas; he always put up a fight.

So one day his mother decided to tell him, "All right, you don't need to get changed. You can just go to preschool in your pajamas, then." She buckled him into the car, they drove off to preschool, and Tommy happily marched into his classroom in his flannel dinosaur pajamas.

When he got there, his teacher looked at him and said, "Oh, Tommy, we do not wear our pajamas to class. Pajamas are for sleeping, and here we have to wear big-boy clothes." For the rest of the day the kids in his class laughed at him because he was wearing his pajamas at preschool.

Tommy always got dressed after that.

Natural consequences are a powerful tool for parents. One of the reasons they're so effective is that the children have to face the consequences of their actions without the parent imposing any. That's what Tommy's mother found with their pajama debacle.

I found in my interviews that parents of kids who didn't rebel often used natural consequences to teach their children valuable lessons. Heidi is one of those examples. She didn't have a pattern of rebellion in high school and had a great relationship with each of her parents. Her family isn't religious, and near the end of high school her parents started letting her go to some parties. They had rules about how to drink responsibly, and they made it very clear that they expected her to use discretion.

"My parents were very logical," Heidi explained, "so when

they told me not to do something, they also told me why. When it came to partying, it was the same way. I was allowed to go to only a few parties, and if I wanted to go, I often had to go as the designated driver because my parents didn't want me to get into the habit of drinking in high school.

"My parents were very strict about safe drinking," Heidi told me, "so they didn't want me getting drunk. There was one time, though, where I went to a party and I drank too much. I was sick the next day and felt awful. I told my dad how horrible I was feeling, and all I wanted was a big hug and lots of sympathy. But instead my dad said, 'I'm glad you realize drinking too much wasn't smart. Now, time to get up or you're going to be late for work.' I told him I was going to call in sick because I didn't feel good. Instead of agreeing with my plan, he said, 'Well, that's too bad, but you did this to yourself. You can't call in sick because of a choice you made. So get up and go to work.'"

Heidi laughed. "I was so mad that he made me go to work hung over, but it really made the lesson stick."

IS SPANKING THE ONLY CULPRIT?

Looking at the negative effects of spanking and the positive effects of discipline techniques such as natural consequences, it can be tempting to think that all forms of discipline that impose consequences to behavior are healthy as long as it's not spanking. But that doesn't seem to be the case. Many of the people I interviewed who rebelled, even if they weren't spanked, were exposed to much harsher forms of discipline than we who didn't rebel were. Here are some examples:

- "I was constantly grounded in high school. And no, I wasn't a good kid, but I was punished even for really little things—if I talked back to Mom, for example, I would be grounded for a week. It really didn't seem very fair."
- "My mom had the funniest discipline. She would take away our privileges if we didn't listen to her. If we argued with her, we lost our right to talk. So we weren't allowed to talk anymore. And she'd interrupt us any time we tried to. And if we weren't downstairs on time for breakfast, she'd take away our phones for days. It was pretty strict in our house."
- "The main form of discipline I had in high school was my mom taking away things I had been looking forward to for weeks. If I mouthed off to Mom, didn't clean my room, or did something else small like that, she would take away the car so that I couldn't go visit my friends or go on a youth trip. Although I did something wrong, I was punished much too harshly, and I would just explode—it didn't seem fair."

The difference between these forms of discipline and the consequences that Heidi or Tommy faced was that the consequences Heidi's and Tommy's parents used fit the crime. They naturally occurred from the behavior—they were fair.

The kinds of consequences we who didn't rebel had were put in place not to punish us as much as to help us learn *why* the behavior was bad. It was a teaching method instead of just another way to stop the behavior. Our parents had the same mind-set that Dylan's parents did: it was their job to help train our character, not just stop bad behavior. The kids who did rebel, though, were faced with consequences that seemed very unfair. And when they were presented with consequences that didn't match the action, the lesson was lost in the injustice of it all.

GOOD CHARACTER RATHER THAN GOOD BEHAVIOR ALONE

My sister and I are two very different people. When I was young, if I got caught writing on the walls with crayon, all my parents had to do was say, "That's a bad thing to do," and the guilt alone was enough to stop me from ever doing the behavior again. Katie was very different. Katie would be writing happily on the wall with crayon and she'd see Mom or Dad coming. So she'd put down her crayon, hang her head, and start bawling, "I'm a bad girl! I'm so sorry! I'll never do it again!" and then she'd put herself in a time-out.

The minute my parents' backs were turned, however, she'd wipe her eyes and go back to cheerfully coloring on the same wall as before. My parents realized Katie wasn't going to respond to discipline the same way I did and that she often required actual consequences as well as conversations to get the point across. She had a lot more time-outs and a lot more natural consequences enforced than I did, that's for sure.

When discipline is tailored to the child rather than to the act alone, it allows parents to develop their children's character by focusing on each child's needs, not just on stopping the behavior. This is the approach taken by every parent of the kids I interviewed who didn't rebel.

That is where the problem with spanking lies. Spanking is not discipline—it's a punishment. Its entire focus is on stopping bad behavior rather than shaping good character.

As Christians, our ultimate goal is to raise children who are going to run after God with all their hearts. So why not start seeing moments of misbehavior as opportunities to teach children, instead of as problems that need to be controlled? I think that sounds like a good place to start.

7

REALITY-BASED PARENTING

CHASING GOD, NOT GOLD

When Jenny was twelve, she discovered Broadway. She would belt out the soundtracks of all her favorite musicals day and night around the house. At one point, she asked her mom, "If I had singing lessons, do you think I could become a Broadway singer?"

The problem: Jenny had a voice only a mother could love. And her mom—well, she didn't particularly love it either, so she wasn't keen on paying for singing lessons on a tight budget when her daughter lacked talent. She'd much rather sign her up for dance or piano. So her mom said, "Well, Jenny, I don't think that Broadway is a good fit, but isn't it fun just to sing?" Jenny signed up for dance instead and excelled, becoming a dance teacher in high school while continuing to belt out ballads in the shower.

Jenny's mom didn't push her daughter toward areas in which she couldn't succeed; she pushed her toward areas where she would. She had a realistic appraisal of her daughter's talent and led Jenny toward a high school career that helped her save up for her first year of college tuition.

The ability to cope with the realities of life is a skill many adults lack, especially adults in the millennial generation. On my first day of university classes, for example, my university professors had to make disclaimers that they would not accept calls from angry parents of students who only got a D on their last test. That's right: parents calling professors to make sure their kids never had to experience failure was enough of a problem that my professor had to make an official announcement about it. I remember thinking how completely ridiculous that was, especially since everyone was at least eighteen or nineteen.

Parents are great at celebrating when their kid rises above— but what about when they're just average, or even below average? Surely a child's success in life can't be contingent on being number one. After all, failure is unavoidable. We can't all be great at everything. By definition, 99 percent of children will never be in that top 1 percent. Yet we seem unable to truly grasp that concept—we see moms pushing their kids to enter singing competitions and talent shows when it's obvious to everyone else that they'll never make it. We see parents calling in to university professors, complaining about their adult child's grade.

Psychologists have found that if you poll a random group of people and ask them, "Do you think you are below average, average, or above average?" In any task, the majority of people will say they are above average. Which is, frankly, impossible. We have a warped idea of our abilities and seem to be predisposed to avoid admitting that we have limitations. And we see parents shielding their children from failure again and again so they never have to feel that they aren't number one.

But what if having a realistic view of who God made your kids to be and accepting their limitations helps kids cope better with real life?

One of the characteristics I found among others who didn't rebel was the ability to see oneself realistically and thus prepare to face the real world. We didn't live believing we were that top 1 percent, but we understood what God made us good at and what He didn't. Many kids don't have that ability because they are sheltered from any and all failure their entire childhood. When they enter the real world, it all comes crashing down.

Physical flexibility has never been my strong suit, to put it mildly. I threw out my back for the first time when I was only nine. Balance has always been a challenge too. Not only do I frequently trip going downstairs, but for years it was a running joke in our family how I could also fall *up* stairs. Most kids are clumsy around age twelve and then level out after their growth spurt. I did not. My parents put my younger sister (who had been doing splits and handstands since kindergarten) in gymnastics, but not me. I got to do Highland dancing. It seemed safer, with my lack of ability in flexibility and balance. Only after I had signed up did we realize that a great part of Highland dancing is dancing on swords, but by that point it was too late—I was hooked.

And I was okay with accepting defeat in gymnastics because I grew up in a family where my mother always laughed about how bad she was at sports and my dad always laughed about how he couldn't sing. Sometimes you're just not the best at something—and that's okay. In fact, one summer when I asked my mom if I could join the same competitive soccer team as a friend, she told me frankly that I wouldn't make it through the tryouts. And she was right—so instead, I played on the homeschoolers' soccer team the next summer. At the same time, I qualified for the internationals team in Bible Quizzing and received awards for my piano playing. I knew what I was good at, and I worked at it.

One of the most recent busts in social psychology is the self-esteem movement. The premise goes like this: kids who get good grades in school tend to have higher self-esteem.[1] Therefore, if we raise kids' self-esteem, we can raise academic performance. Great idea, right?

That's what education experts thought in the late 1980s, and they brought self-esteem-based teaching programs into hundreds of schools across the United States and Canada. Teachers were trained to continuously praise children, saying things like, "You are so smart, Sally!" and "You are so good at reading!" even when the kids made mistakes. The thought was that if they felt good enough about themselves, they would be motivated to work through problem areas and would learn more effectively.

Turns out they were wrong. In the end, this wound up being a problem of misunderstanding the correlation—the fact that kids with good grades have high self-esteem does not imply that children with high self-esteem will get good grades. Instead, research has found that praising effort rather than innate ability is what helps kids do well.

This is what a study by Claudia Mueller and Carol Dweck

found. Mueller and Dweck presented kids with a puzzle, and then each child was praised for his or her success either because the child had worked hard at it (effort) or because he or she was simply very smart (innate ability).[2] Then they presented the children with a choice for another puzzle—one that was easy and would make them look smart or one that was harder and would require them to learn and stretch themselves. What they found was that children who were praised for intelligence after they succeeded on the first puzzle chose the easy puzzles that would make them look smart, at the expense of learning. Children who were praised for effort, on the other hand, chose the harder puzzle that would require them to stretch themselves.[3] In addition, kids who were praised for intelligence did not handle failure as well as kids who had been praised for effort, since they attributed their success or failure to a lack of ability rather than a lack of effort.[4] So rather than saying "You are so smart," it's better to say "Great job working through that. I know that was tough, but you sounded it out and got there in the end."

Study after study has repeated these findings. Simply telling everyone that they are wonderful and special and smart doesn't lead to better achievement. Instead, it makes kids unwilling to work through failure. And as we all well know, failure is an inescapable part of life.

Despite knowing that kids can't be perfect in everything, however, many parents are terrified to say that their kids are anything but the best. When I taught swimming lessons, there were some parents who would become positively irate whenever I didn't pass one of their children to the next swimming level.

They'd hide the report cards and try to keep their child from figuring out that they hadn't passed—which inevitably made finding out they were still at the same level next time around that much harder on the kid.

Most of us realize at some time or another that we're not the best at everything. Those of us who don't are probably narcissists. For some of us, it's when we're in fourth grade and we realize we're never going to be good soccer players. For others, it's in high school when we're struggling to get the grades everyone else is. For still others, it's in university when we've been one of the best for twenty years of our lives and for the first time we're struggling. And we all get through it. But some people come through it with more scars than others.

The stories of Michael and Amelia can give us some insight into why.

WHEN YOU FIND OUT YOU'RE NOT THE BEST

When I met Michael, he was in his third year of biomed and struggling with his faith. I tried to help him reconnect with the Christian community, but he never seemed interested. As a high school student, he had been on top of the world—he got As in all his classes, was captain of the soccer team, and dated the prettiest girl in the school. He was one of the "it" kids in his church's youth group. All through his life he had never failed—largely because his parents made sure he didn't.

Michael was fortunate to be naturally smart, but in high school his mom edited all his papers for him, and his dad corrected his math and science homework before he handed it in. Of course, they went over their edits with him to help him learn, but Michael joked with me about how he could get his mom to do his entire assignment for him if he played it right. His parents would coo and fuss whenever he brought back another excellent grade, and he thought of himself as the "smart kid."

In his mom's eyes, in particular, Michael could do nothing wrong. In eighth grade Michael was on a swimming team for a while and really enjoyed it. He was only middle of the pack, though, and one day the coach passed over Michael when it came to choosing which of the swimmers went to the regional meet. When his mother found out, she immediately pulled her son from the swim team. Michael described that car ride home as tense—the idea that anyone saw her son as anything but the best had infuriated his mom. For the first time Michael experienced failure, and from his mother's expression he felt that failure should bring shame.

When he told his family he wanted to go into medicine, they were thrilled—being a doctor was the perfect profession for their brilliant son. They sent him off to university with well wishes and high hopes. He was smart, and he was a good Christian kid—he'd thrive at university.

Or so they thought. Michael went to his first semester filled with hope and excitement for this next chapter in life. After the first midterm season, his average was about a 70—not bad, but not what he was used to receiving. He told me that the first year depressed him greatly when he couldn't maintain his scholarship and get those eighties and nineties that came so easily in high school.

At the same time, he had been paired up with a roommate who was heavily into the party scene. Michael started drinking with his roommate in their dorm, then started going to parties. He didn't feel like the smart kid anymore and, in his search for identity, he turned to the party crowd since they made him feel accepted and it helped distract him.

As the years went on, his grades kept slipping and he started drinking more to cope with the failure he'd never had to deal with before. By the end of third year he was on academic probation, had gotten into a habit of partying and sleeping around, and decided to drop out of the program and move back with his parents to retake control of his life and of his faith.

I remember that when we talked about why he was leaving school, he told me, "I just don't know who I am. I'm the smart kid and I'm dropping out. I don't know how this happened."

ACCEPTING FAILURE AS A PATH TO FREEDOM

I met Amelia when I was twelve. My family had just switched churches, and I was pretty scared when we stepped through the door of the new church. But fourteen-year-old Amelia enveloped Katie and me in a big hug and introduced herself. From that day on, Amelia was my role model: she was older than me, she had

Disney-princess hair, and she could even sing as loudly as I could (which, as anyone who knows me can tell you, is quite a feat).

Amelia grew up with a very competitive spirit. What comes naturally to Amelia is to work and work and work until you see the results you want. Why would you ever admit defeat?

This perfectionist streak started young. In fifth grade Amelia's youth group decided to throw a mini Olympics. It contained the typical types of games and sports—beanbag tosses, races, and soccer, to name a few. Amelia's competitive side got very excited about this, despite the fact that she hated sports of any kind. She rallied her team, and they tried their hardest all day.

And she placed second.

"My little perfectionist self was devastated," Amelia said, laughing.

A few days later Amelia was still very upset, and her mom asked her what was wrong. Amelia replied, "We came in second, so we might as well have lost. We're losers." Amelia's mom, however, had a different opinion.

"Whoa," her mom said. "First off, second place is not losing. You did great, but if you had come in fourth, it would also have been okay. In fact, if you had come in last, it would have been okay too. You were not there to win. You were there to have a really good time. Did you have fun?"

Amelia begrudgingly agreed that they had, and although she didn't internalize the message at that moment, her mom and dad continually reminded her that it's okay not to be the best.

When she started at university many years later, she had high hopes. Always one of the brightest kids in her class back in high school, she was accepted into a prestigious university to study biology, one of her passions. But as prepared as she thought she was, classes were a shock. She wasn't the big fish in a little pond anymore—she found herself a small fish in a big pond. She was surrounded by the best-of-the-best science students in Canada, competing for top of the class with students who were, quite frankly, smarter than she was. She had to deal with not being the best.

"I did feel a lot of pressure," Amelia explained, "but it was mainly from myself. I always knew that my parents were proud of me even if I didn't get the highest grade."

In her second month of her first semester, she failed a test for the first time. It came as a shock. Although she brought her grade up in that course during the rest of the semester, that first test was a huge turning point in Amelia's life. "I was devastated by that test," Amelia explained. She called her mom, distraught. Her mom, however, didn't try to convince Amelia that her grades would improve. Rather, she told her daughter, "You will not succeed at everything. And that's perfectly fine. You don't have to be the best at everything; you just need to do your best and let God take care of the rest. Make sure you don't sacrifice your well-being for your grades—God has equipped you for what He has planned for you."

So Amelia, despite her perfectionism, decided that she needed to let go of her dream of having the highest marks in her class. "I decided that getting the best mark wasn't most important to me. I wanted to have time to be involved with Christian fellowship groups and to keep up with friends, and I just didn't have time for both." Amelia shrugged. "So I worked my hardest, but I was never top of a class again."

Overall, Amelia achieved good marks—she passed her classes, and she graduated with her degree in biology and was accepted for a master's in biology as well. About a year in, she realized that her master's degree was not what she wanted to be doing. It wasn't an easy decision, since quitting meant failure in Amelia's eyes, but eventually she admitted she wasn't where she was called and left it behind.

When Amelia was faced with threats to her identity as the smart one, it didn't shake her faith. That's because for Amelia, the biggest part of her identity was never her grades. Instead, her parents had raised her to know that her identity was found in Christ alone, and in who He was and what He did for her. They would say prayers together every night, and as part of their ritual Amelia's mom and dad would say "I love you," and then ask Amelia, "Why do I love you?"

And Amelia would answer, "Because I am a gift from God."

Today Amelia is embarking on a new chapter. She has been accepted into a prestigious midwifery program, and I can't picture anyone who is better suited for it. She is not where she thought she was going to be when she was sixteen, but she knows that God is pleased with her, and that is all that really matters.

REALIZING SECOND DOESN'T MEAN LAST

Failure often seems like the end of the world, and since we live in a culture that demands perfection, anything less than perfect is deemed a failure. Unfortunately, we are simply not able to be perfect in every single way. An inability to cope with this can lead to something called *all-or-nothing thinking*, which is found among people with a variety of mental illnesses, including depression, anxiety, and various eating disorders. All-or-nothing thinking distorts reality so we can't see that even if we aren't on top, we're still doing pretty well. And it doesn't understand that not being on top isn't the end of the world. It's a lot like how little fifth-grade Amelia saw her second-place trophy from the church Olympics—second wasn't first, so it might as well be last.

My parents have always known that I have a perfectionist streak and that it would likely be my downfall. In fact, my perfectionism runs so deep that my third-year psychology class professor used me as an illustration to explain a type A personality to a classroom of one hundred students. Whenever I'd have a panic attack because I might not win at quizzing or not get an A+ in a course, my mom would remind me: "God is responsible for your success. All He requires from you is your effort. And God rewards good effort—but *He* is in charge of the outcome. Not you." And like Amelia, although I've had a hard time owning that message, it has shaped how I respond to failures in my life.

ALLOWING GOD TO SAY WHO IS BEST

During our second year at internationals for quizzing, my sister's team made the finals. It was a huge deal—this was the first time in five years our district had made the top three teams, and they were a real contender. One of the boys from the New York district turned to my mom and jokingly said, "I guess I know who you're praying for!" My mom laughed and said, "Actually, I'm not praying that Katie's team wins. I don't know what God wants. I'm just praying that they all feel like they did their best and that God will let who needs to win, win." He was really surprised, but I wasn't. I was used to her attitude.

Starting when I was nine, my sister and I participated in annual piano competitions. Every time we performed, my mom prayed that whoever used their music to serve God the most would win—not necessarily Katie or me. And we knew that she was praying this. Of course, she *hoped* that it would be us, but it was just common knowledge in our family that if we didn't win, that was also okay, because God might want to use someone other than us.

FOCUSING ON GROWTH, NOT ON GOLD

But sometimes some kids just have it tougher than others when it comes to this quest to be the best. We all have that one friend who can just ace a final without studying or jump into any sporting game and dominate. And life can often seem very easy for those kids, relatively speaking. It's easy to encourage kids when they're doing well, but how do you encourage kids when they have a harder time? Can you find that balance between encouraging them to keep trying without expecting them to triumph?

I say yes. As those self-esteem studies show us, the point of reality-based parenting is that parents praise effort, not results. This builds up something psychologists call *grit*—the ability to stick with it even when your actions aren't yielding any results. And grit, according to recent research, seems to be more predictive of success than any other trait.[5] Higher levels of grit make it more likely that high school students will graduate on time, cadets will make it through the first year of training, and new teachers will stick through the first year and become more effective than teachers with low grit.[6] The ability to push through even when you aren't on top, or aren't getting the medals, is what helps you achieve your goals in the long term. And families with children who didn't rebel know this.

- "Although I knew my parents wanted the best from me, it wasn't about being on top; it was about working hard. They didn't only focus on our grades, but also on how hard we tried."

- "I hated practicing piano. It was a fight every day for three years, but my parents kept telling me, 'Even if you're never the best, you've got to stick with it because one day you're going to love to be able to just play.' And now I do love it and play every day to de-stress from my college classes, and I'm glad I didn't give up."

- "My parents were really encouraging whenever I worked hard at my job, even though I had to miss a lot of social events because of it. I needed the money for school, so they told me they were proud that I didn't give up."

TEACHING KIDS THE
VALUE OF WORKING HARD

My summer camp friend Amanda grew up as the oldest in a big, happy, Christian family. One of her biggest struggles, however, was her ADHD.

"I had to work extra hard to get above a B or a C grade," Amanda explained. "I wanted to do well so badly that I would become inconsolable if I got anything below a 70 and was angry with myself for anything below an eighty. But often I just had to work ten times harder than the other kids in my class."

Amanda's parents did a great job of encouraging Amanda academically while taking into consideration how her ADHD created difficulty for her. Amanda remembers her dad saying to her, "You just have to work the best you can, but at some point you have to learn how to let go and accept that your best is all you can do—your mental health and your sleep are more important than a good grade." That said, they also expected that she would do well in school. They knew she was capable of getting good grades, even if she didn't become the school valedictorian. Whenever she brought back a good grade, her dad would congratulate her and scoop her up in a big bear hug. And if she came home with a bad grade, devastated with her mark, they would ask, "Amanda, did you try your best?"

"Yes," Amanda would reply.

"Then you have nothing to be ashamed of. Sometimes you have ups; sometimes things are just difficult and your best is all you can do. You tried hard, we're proud of you, and we know you're going to do great things. Just keep on at it, and God will open the doors He has for you."

Amanda's parents' response to her success as well as her failures helped build up a positive work ethic, and not just in academics. Amanda had been involved in her city's skating league since she was seven. She was extremely passionate about skating and skated competitively until she was thirteen. However, she never placed first, and each competition launched a roller coaster of emotions. Her parents, seeing how much not winning was hurting Amanda, sat her down one day and said, "Amanda, we're concerned that there is too much pressure on you with skating right now. We don't want you to quit because you're not winning. Skating is great exercise and it produces perseverance. But we don't think that competitions are a good idea because you're so focused on winning it's not making skating any fun."

Amanda continued to skate after that, and her excitement for the sport was reignited. "I kept skating until I injured my ankle when I was sixteen," Amanda told me, "and I worked just as hard after I quit competitions as I did before. It was so freeing to be able to just skate without having to worry about the competition of it all—I was able to skate simply because I loved it."

Today Amanda is attending college and starting up her own jewelry business, all while running Bible studies with her college's Christian club. Starting a business is hard, and the perseverance she learned from skating is helping her keep going even when it gets tough—and that's better than any gold medal.

IT'S NOT ABOUT WINNING—IT'S ABOUT HOW YOU PLAY THE GAME

In Matthew 25 Jesus tells a parable of three men whose master leaves them with different sums of money to look after while he's gone. One man is given one talent, another is given two talents, and the last man is given five talents. Now, in the parable the men with two and five talents both go and invest the money, and by the time the master comes back, they have doubled his money. But the man with one talent goes and hides his money, because he is afraid of his master, and the money does not see any growth.

We spend a lot of time focusing on the man with one talent and the man with five talents, but in my experience we don't talk a lot about the man with two talents. But something I've realized is this: the master was equally pleased with the man with two talents and the man with five. He gave them both the same praise: "Well done, good and faithful servant; you have been faithful over a little, I will set you over much; enter into the joy of your master" (Matt. 25:21, 23 RSV). It wasn't about how much they made—it was about how they used what they were given.

I think that's where we go wrong a lot of the time. Michael's mom thought that unless he was a five-talent guy, it wasn't worth trying. Amelia's and Amanda's moms, though, knew that it wasn't about how many talents you were given—it was about how you used them. It was about understanding the love and acceptance of God and working your hardest to be a good and faithful servant for Him.

Maybe we all need to start Amelia's bedtime ritual. "I love you," said her parents. "And why do I love you?" And she would answer, "Because I am a gift from God." It isn't about how much. It's about how.

8

IT'S ABOUT GOD, NOT THE CHURCH

YOU DON'T GET STARS FOR ATTENDANCE

On Sunday mornings when I was five, I would hop out of the minivan and run to the heavy church doors, tugging with all my might, because on the other side of the door were adults who, in my mind, were waiting with bated breath to talk to me. I know now there may have been some other reasons for their presence in that building, but my little five-year-old brain thought it all revolved around me. Mr. Heidt would bend down and say hello, Mrs. Willows gushed over my missing front teeth, and Mrs. Fox always gave me a star for knowing my verses. I would saunter into the church, and adults who were not my family loved me. It was the safest place I knew. Plus, it didn't hurt that they all told me how cute I was.

At my university (the University of Ottawa), many of my psychology professors are pro church even though they themselves are not Christians, since they know that being part of a church community is beneficial to adolescents. Studies show that being part of a religious group decreases the risk of depression, suicidal ideology, antisocial behavior, and substance abuse.[1] It also decreases the likelihood that girls will get involved in risky sexual behavior.[2] When I heard about these studies and thought back to my own experiences, I started wondering what aspect of religion was the key to this positive behavior.

I want to tell the stories here of two men I know from university—Ethan and Patrick. Both were raised in two-parent households with sisters. Both excelled at sports and academics, and both dated in high school. Both had families who were extremely involved in church, and both from a very young age volunteered to help on a regular basis. On a surface level, they seemed to have completely parallel lives.

However, there is one big difference: only Patrick rebelled.

So what went wrong?

A TALE OF TWO FAMILIES

Lisa Miller and Murav Gur studied the trends between religiosity and sexual behavior. They found that personal devotion to religion is what had the greatest likelihood of predicting that someone was less likely to be sexually irresponsible.[3] In fact, it was such a powerful factor that if you increased a participant's personal devotion by only one unit, there was a 7 percent drop in the likelihood that they would engage in nonromantic sexual activity. The question becomes, "How do we nurture personal devotion in our teens?" Our default answer is usually "Let's go to church more!"

When we see a kid who goes off the rails, often we think that the solution is more church. In the words of the classic *Saturday Night Live* skit, they just need more cowbell. But what if there is something else going on? What if it's not church attendance per se, but the commitment level to God that matters?

Many of us have heard the expression "Going to church makes you a Christian as much as sitting in a garage makes you a car." I fear some parents believe that cliché applies to adults but not to kids. Even if the kid is dragged to church kicking and screaming, these parents believe that Sunday morning worship is the cure-all for teenage rebellion. And if that doesn't work, send them off to a few youth retreats!

Interestingly enough, though, Miller and Gur's study doesn't indicate that more church alone will help. Instead, the researchers drew a very clear distinction between teens who were personally dedicated to their beliefs (those with high personal devotion) and those who were extremely rigid in them (those with high personal conservatism). The difference between the two is subtle but vital. A teen with high personal conservatism is very rules oriented—he or she has dos and don'ts for everything, and that teen's faith is often based around authority figures other than Christ. For instance, with conservative families the children are taught that the father has the last say on any topic, and crossing him is wrong and disrespectful. Breaking the rules is unthinkable, often leading to all-or-nothing thinking. The rules aren't even necessarily wrong or bad—they're just very strict, and that's where the danger lies. Personal devotion, on the other hand, is when the beliefs and values of the religion have become an integral part of your life without the obsession with rule adherence—even though these kids also tend to follow the rules. The difference is where the emphasis is.

Think of a sixteen-year-old girl who's saving herself for marriage. A girl who is extremely devoted to her beliefs but not highly personally conservative may kiss a boy whom she realizes isn't a good guy and then feel it was a silly thing to do, but won't beat herself up about it. She decides not to pursue the relationship and carries along on her merry way. If a girl has extremely high conservatism, though, and kisses a boy who turns out to be a bad guy, she may feel that she's no longer pure. Instead of breaking it off, she goes further with him because she already feels like damaged goods.

This type of scenario is probably why the researchers found that while personal devotion lowered the risk for unhealthy sexual behavior, stronger personal fundamentalism did not lead to less sexual activity. In fact, personal conservatism was linked to riskier sexual behavior. Miller and Gur posited that this may be due to the emphasis on submitting to all kinds of authority in the beliefs of fundamentalist communities, as well as this all-or-nothing approach that many conservative teenagers adopt when it comes to sin.[4] This contrast between attendance and personal devotion is not unique to this study either. Another study done in 2008 by Kyle C. Longest and Stephen Vaisey studied the effects that religious behavior had on marijuana use in teenagers and found that unless the kids chose religion for themselves, no amount of religion would make them steer clear of drugs.

> We find that if a young person does not internalize religious teachings (to the point that they are used as a basis for making decisions) or does not form intergenerational connections based around shared religious beliefs, involvement in religion may simply provide more opportunities to begin using marijuana.[5]

Wow. More church doesn't help much at all if there's nothing under the surface. And that makes sense when I look at my friends Ethan and Patrick. More church didn't help Patrick; in fact, the more church he got, the more he ran away from God. For Ethan, though, church cemented his belief.

To understand the difference, let's take a look at Ethan's story first.

ETHAN: WHEN CHURCH GOES WELL

Ethan was part of a family that experienced church as a refreshing community—a place where their family could recharge and rest.

"My church experience was pretty great," Ethan recounted to me. "I grew up going to a small church with a few kids my own age—two of my best friends went there too. The church had a fair deal of kids' activities when I was younger, like kids' club stuff during the week or youth groups. But the best thing," he told me, "was the old people. They just have such an interest in hearing how you're doing, and then will give you one-liners of wisdom."

Hmm. Remember what the researchers said about intergenerational connections? Sounds like there may have been something to that. Just like little five-year-old me running to the church door.

As Ethan hit his teenage years, the kids from his church became his best friends. He's also very musically gifted, so during his sophomore year of high school he started volunteering with the worship team, playing the piano. Becoming part of the community and living out their gifts was what held importance to his family—it was about how they could serve and not what the church could give them. "We were encouraged to volunteer even if we weren't getting anything out of it. We were told to use our gifts to give back."

That said, even though Ethan's parents have shown their son what it means to try to live a good Christian life, they were never "super-Christians," as Ethan puts it.

"They're not over-the-top," Ethan explained, "but it's a natural consistency. I know many families whose parents are excellent Christians, and I think my parents want to be that, so they do their best. But I wouldn't say I come from a super-Christian home." They didn't debate predestination at the dinner table. Ethan isn't even sure his parents know what the debate would be. They didn't do family devotions or pray for missionaries together. They didn't even really pray out loud that often. But his parents showed their dedication in more subtle ways.

"My parents invested in their Christian community. They took turns hosting their small group. They worked on their personal walks too. I'd wake up and see devotional books on the counter after they'd gone to work and know that they'd been reading their Bibles."

Ethan's parents also encouraged him to get involved in groups with kids his own age—in fact, his best friends through high school were from his church. "I have three or four best friends who were guys who were all in my year at school. We'd go camping, hiking, and really let out our nerdy side when we were together, with frequent talks about *Lord of the Rings* and *Star Wars* in mass proportion. Sometimes we'd just go into the backyard and shoot squirrels with pellet guns. Just silly stuff."

By the time he started university, Christian community and church had become such a huge part of his life that when a friend from camp invited him to be a part of IVCF (InterVarsity Christian Fellowship, one of the Christian groups on campus) it was an easy decision. "I was at camp after grade twelve," Ethan recalled, "and a girl walked up to me and said, 'Ethan! I hear you're going into music. I'm in music! I hear you're a Christian. I'm a Christian! Join my Bible study!' And with those three statements I said sure, because I knew I wanted to be involved with something that would challenge me."

When I asked him more about why he wanted to get involved in a Christian group on campus, Ethan told me a lot of it was about shaping who he was as an adult. "I wanted to do

WHY I DIDN'T REBEL

something Christian, because when you come to university from high school, it's very much a reforming of your identity, and I knew I wouldn't be defined by my athletic abilities anymore, and my grades (to the same extent) wouldn't be an identity thing either. I was figuring out who I was going to be in university."

He chose to be involved in the Christian group because he wanted to have his identity where it really counts—in Christ. By his second year in university, he was leading Bible studies, and by the end of third year, he was on the leadership team. Now he is still involved in that same church and has begun to lead worship, too, not only play in the background.

PATRICK: WHEN CHURCH SENDS YOU RUNNING FROM GOD

Patrick and I became friends my first year at university. He and my friend Brooke were from the same hometown and attended the same church growing up. The three of us started hanging out together, having Netflix marathons, because Brooke was trying to save Patrick from himself. She knew he needed more Christian friends, so she recruited me to keep him from the party scene.

One day, when I asked Brooke to describe Patrick at church, she laughed. "Well, once he helped me teach the kindergarten's Sunday school. It was a disaster—I came back from taking some of the girls to the washroom, and I saw him standing there in an empty classroom, terror on his face, saying, 'I don't know where the boys went. They were right here. Now they're gone.' I had to chase the rest of the four-year-olds for about ten minutes before they would all stay in the room. I didn't really ask him to help me out again after that."

Patrick's a great guy now. He's one of my best guy friends from school. He has gotten involved in church and volunteers with Big Brothers. Who he is now, though, is not the same as who he was in high school, or even in his first year of university. In his freshman year he was deep into the party scene, involved in drinking, sex, recreational drugs, and even vandalism. He got into quite a bit of trouble in high school, too, even though he was involved in church his whole life.

As Brooke explains, "I can tell you two things with absolute certainty: that boy went to church, and that boy got into a lot of trouble."

Ironically, Patrick's parents were more involved in their church than Ethan's parents were in theirs, but rather than strengthening Patrick's faith, his parents' involvement made him more frustrated with Christianity.

Patrick's parents were the super-Christians that Ethan's parents were not. They *did* debate predestination at the dinner table—though it was less of a debate than it was Patrick's father telling everyone what their family believed. Patrick's dad served on the church board, led the men's ministry, and hosted Bible study groups in his home. He led every fund-raiser and sang on the worship team. Patrick, though, did not see the values that his dad was being praised for preaching at church being lived out at home.

"My parents' work brought a lot of stress home, and there

was a link missing between understanding the love of Christ and them showing it to other people," Patrick explained in our meeting. Work was a duty to provide for the family, and the church had the same feel. Church was about gaining respect and doing the right thing, but it was lacking the community and honesty that Ethan's home had to offer. To Patrick, "it just didn't seem like it was a vibrant, authentic, all-in kind of Christianity where they were bold and full of the fruits of the Spirit. They weren't joyful because of God, but more felt the weight of work that was involved with serving God."

Patrick's parents modeled that going to church and "having it all together" was what mattered. If people were coming over, they would not rest until everything was tidy and perfect. Only the best clothes could be worn on Sundays. If anyone challenged his parents or tried to correct them, it was taken as a personal attack. Respect for one's parents was instilled in them as a vital element of the Christian life—and it was defined as agreeing with his parents on everything.

When Patrick was in high school, the gay marriage debate was hitting the news here in Canada. Patrick piped up one night at dinner, saying, "I just don't understand—if two people really love each other, why is it so bad?"

His father slammed down his fork and, shoving a finger into Patrick's face, shouted, "This is a respectable family, and this family does not accept or condone such sinful things! No child of mine will ever accept gay marriage."

Patrick remembers thinking, *But I just asked a question.* From then on, he kept his questions to himself.

Patrick remembers frequent yelling matches over even the tiniest of things. "There was extreme anger from Dad if we did anything wrong—yelling and the like—and generally it seemed like he was overreacting." All the screaming matches coupled with the intense stress from work and church involvement resulted in parenting that seemed out of control, Patrick explained. It wasn't about mentoring or teaching the kids anything; it was about keeping a lid on the stress. Even though their dad had a successful business, for instance, he would never take Patrick to work with him to show him around because that would have meant more work for his dad. If Patrick had a track-and-field meet, he was only praised if he won; if he didn't, his father mumbled about how he had wasted so much time on him that could have been spent at work.

Patrick hadn't witnessed the love he kept hearing about in church in his own home, and because of that, he hadn't learned how to rely on family and friends for support when he was struggling with sin, since even the tiniest infraction resulted in another heated fight. By the time high school came, he was fighting temptation solely through his own willpower, which of course does not work. Eventually, his resolve gave out. He hadn't found what he was looking for, so he threw in the towel, stopped following God, and started his deep descent into the party scene.

Here's the scary thing: Patrick *wanted* to be a Christian. My heart broke when Patrick recounted his struggles throughout his childhood. "When I reached puberty," he explained, "sexual sin started hitting me, and when I got to high school, it was hopeless. There was never an end, and I didn't see there ever

WHY I DIDN'T REBEL

being an end, so I decided to give up. Grade twelve and my first year of university, I said to myself, 'I'm giving up on Christianity because it's just too hard.'" And then he ended up where he was at the beginning of this story—drinking, doing drugs, sleeping around, and running far away from God.

That isn't the end of Patrick's story, though. When Patrick left home for university several hours away, he moved into a house of Christian guys his age. He still had his freedom, and during his freshman year he figured he could do anything he wanted to— and he did. But while he was off making his life apart from God, the guys he was living with dragged him to church every week. The church had a dynamic college-and-careers program, which he started attending—mostly to meet girls. Eventually he met more authentic Christians, and he began to think that maybe they had what he had been missing in his life—a true, personal connection to Jesus.

Seeing how strong Patrick is now has been an amazing experience for me, and especially for Brooke, who witnessed both his descent and his salvation now. Looking at his transformation shows one thing in particular about church: how much you serve is not as important as why you serve. Patrick went from a family with parents who were extremely involved in church—but for the wrong reasons—to a house where the guys were involved because they truly wanted to help. And his entire outlook on Christianity changed. Authenticity is more important than appearance. Ethan's parents understood that. Patrick's parents didn't.

Having a good church is a very important tool that God uses to bring people to Him. Being part of that community was crucial for little five-year-old me, as it was for fifteen-year-old Brooke and seventeen-year-old Ethan. The church community is what brought Patrick back to God—as soon as he saw it mixed with a true, authentic faith.

WHEN GOD IS FOUND OUTSIDE THE CHURCH

What happens, though, when you don't have the option to go to a great church? If the perfect combination for children is to have authentic parents at a wonderful church community, then kids without one of the two elements are doomed, right?

Maybe not.

Lily and Jennifer are two of my oldest friends—we met when we were in preschool, and their dad, Bill, and their mom, Stacy, have always been like family to us. I was devastated when they moved to Pennsylvania when I was in the third grade, but we have managed to stay close our whole lives despite the distance. Bill is a bit of a jokester, which has given us some great family lore. For instance, one summer, through a flurry of circumstances, he and my dad ended up dancing in togas, greeting people as they arrived at our summer family camp.

When Lily and Jennifer's family left, they went from my small town to move to an even tinier one—so small, in fact, that the town has no evangelical churches. The closest thing was a mainline church where the average age was something like ninety-seven. The church had very few members, a subpar Sunday school program, no real youth group, outdated worship, and questionable judgments from church leadership. Nevertheless, the family attended, even though it wasn't perfect, because they wanted their daughters to understand the importance of church and to be able to find Jesus even among imperfect leadership.

But they did get into trouble. One Sunday, when the worship was particularly dull, Bill started to pretend to conduct the choir with a wooden spoon he had sneaked in, his wife unaware. They were politely asked to abstain from attending for a few weeks after that one.

You might think that having a dad who challenged church authority would lead to kids who didn't respect the church. With this family, though, something else happened: this family raised two girls who are not only respectful, but are gracious and humble toward authority.

Because we lived so far apart, my sister, Katie, and I only saw Lily and Jennifer at that Christian camp our families both attended every summer. When Lily grew old enough, she began to work as a camp counselor, so I got to watch her in a leadership position.

I loved some parts of camp. I adore anything water related, like kayaking or wind surfing, and they had an adrenaline-rush high dive. The rest of it, though, I hated. One year I broke my toe the first day and was relieved, because that meant I wouldn't have to do any more group activities (but I could still kayak!). I faked asthma, cramps—anything that would keep me from having to run around screaming with 150 other girls. The devotionals, too, were never deep enough for me. Yes, I know that you can always learn from God's Word, no matter how many times you read it, but sometimes things are just plain boring and presented at such a basic level—many campers were new Christians—that I spent most of my time tracking ants.

At one point Lily and I stole away for about an hour to just catch up, and I began moaning to her about all my camp woes. I complained that the activity committee was awful, the devotionals were shallow, and I didn't feel there was any point to me going to camp other than to see her and Jennifer. Then Lily—who had been raised in a home that did not blindly submit to church authority—told me that although she agreed with me, I needed more respect for my leaders.

I will never forget that moment. I was so ashamed of myself, because even though I didn't particularly enjoy many of the things that were going on, Lily's words cut to the core—because she was right. I wasn't respecting my leaders, and she called me out on it.

That doesn't sound like a girl who learned church authority is something to be scoffed at. So what did her parents do to teach her that balance?

God set up the church so that there will be people in authority. Sometimes, though, church authority is just plain bad. Sometimes going to church is painful and some things that happen can make you cringe (like when the entire choir is flat except for those two people who are very sharp). What Bill and Stacy did by allowing their girls to hear them talk about the church frankly, but still with kindness—and to see Bill's crazy antics—was to give their girls the gift of honesty. It's not threatening to challenge what Christians are doing, because what Christians do does not impact who Jesus is. To Patrick, church was presented as an all-or-nothing thing: you respect everything and love everything or you're not a real Christian. When Bill and Stacy admitted to the girls that their church wasn't perfect, though, they were training them in the gift of discernment.

This gift of discernment is what Lily used when she told me I was stubborn and wrong. She had experienced bad leadership, so she was able to tell when the leadership was not actually working against God but was just not meshing with my personal tastes. She would not have been able to make that distinction, though, if her parents had taught her it is always wrong to speak up against authority. Only by acknowledging truth can we speak it.

This was common to many of the stories of kids who didn't rebel—not that the kids had perfect church experiences, but that they could recognize that poor or bad leadership did not reflect on God.

- "There were often fights among the leaders of the Bible Quizzing meets. People wanted the program to look like different things. It added stress, but my parents were always quick to remind us to focus on the reason we were there: to memorize the Bible and meet other great Christian kids."
- "When I was in junior high, there was a huge church split, and it was really hard to watch. But my parents talked about it at home openly and explained to us that people don't always agree, but that it was important to keep God—not the conflict—as the focus."
- "When the youth leader said that he liked me more than

my sister, I felt so offended on my sister's behalf. And I felt betrayed by my youth leader because he was trying to create a division between us. So I went to my mom, confused. And instead of setting it up for me to become bitter toward that leader, she encouraged me to use discernment in that situation, and I realized that you can't trust everyone in authority."

Being able to name what was wrong without giving up on faith was key. But there is one more important thing that Lily's parents did—they didn't give up on the church. Instead, they created their own.

When there are few opportunities for corporate worship available, and none of them is particularly good, sometimes you must create your own. That's what this family did. When they were kicked out of church, or when the leadership had been saying something that really wasn't biblical, Bill and Stacy would host home church in their basement with Christian families across the town. They would sing songs, read devotions, and have communion together. When I asked Lily about it, she described her family's faith as hinging on Matthew 18:20, which reads: "For where two or three gather in my name, there am I with them."

When they came to visit the Easter weekend when I was twelve, we experienced home church with them. My parents woke us up and bundled us into our winter coats (it may have been Easter, but this was Canada), and we sat on a dock at six thirty in the morning, the mist rising off the bay. We sang hymns, read the crucifixion and resurrection stories, and took communion together while shivering. It was quiet, simple, and peaceful. There were only eight people there, but God really was in that moment. It's still one of my favorite Easter memories.

"Looking back," Lily explained, "my sister and I do have some disappointment in our experiences growing up in that church. But our parents gave us the ability to see the situation clearly, both the bad and the good. We saw the mistakes that the elders made, and I am forever grateful that my parents created a separate Christian community for us. But primarily we think about the women from that church who mentored us and gave us hugs on Christmas Eve. And about reading all the books in the church library. That ability to see both sides is mainly from my mom, who discussed the church but never said anything bad about anyone, while still staying honest about the situation.

"My parents saw what the church could be doing better," Lily explained, "so they created the home church. But they didn't slander the church we attended. Instead, they taught us that people aren't perfect, so they are going to hurt you at times. It's okay to respond to hurtful things people do, but it's never good to give up on imperfect people, because without them, how can you ever hope to find community?"

This family took God seriously and was able to separate Him from the building of the church. God exists in the church, yes, but He also exists outside of it, and that is something Lily and Jennifer truly learned. Now both of them are involved in Christian campus ministries, and I can safely say that they are true warriors for their faith.

Look at the difference between Lily's family and Patrick's— one was so obsessed with making sure their children knew God that they were willing to give up their status; the other was so obsessed with status that their child didn't truly know God.

HONESTY WITH RESPECT

Remember my story from chapter 1, when I tried to overturn church leadership at barely fifteen? I wished so many times that I could just let it be and allow it to sort itself out on its own, but I just couldn't bring myself to do it. My parents had taught me the lesson of honesty. They had always been up-front with Katie and me when they didn't agree with someone. That taught me to figure out whom I should and should not agree with.

The Bible is full of warnings against false prophets and false teachers, but when kids aren't allowed to question church authority, they aren't trained to be on the watch. My sister and I, on the other hand, were boot camp–style trained to be on guard. For example, my mom was very vocal to us on those car rides home from skating that God cares more about whether or not we're harboring judgment in our hearts than whether or not we're wearing denim. Remember the no-jeans-for-girls mom I told you about in chapter 2? I knew that that particular woman bothered my mom even more than she bothered me. But my mom was always gracious to her—I never saw her make one sarcastic remark toward her (and anyone who knows my mother knows that is quite a feat).

Now, there's a fine line between being honest and being degrading toward church authority. Saying "I can't believe what an idiot Bob is" is quite different from "I'm just not comfortable with a lot of the theology that Bob preaches." My parents modeled the second, never the first. In fact, they would punish me for speaking disrespectfully about anyone. Once, when I was around nine, my parents were in the middle of a conflict with someone on the church board. To try and lend them moral support, I piped up and said, "Don't worry, Daddy. He's just stupid." I fully expected my dad to agree with me, but instead he said, "Rebecca, we don't talk about people like that. We don't agree, but that doesn't mean he's stupid."

That mentality freed me to be able to look and judge for myself and gave me the courage to speak up when I felt that the church leaders were misrepresenting the gospel. When you're allowed to say that you don't agree, you give yourself permission to think and explore your faith on your own—that's when faith travels from appearance to authenticity.

My parents also talked a ton about doctrine—and quite frequently it was to say that they didn't know what they believed. We would debate predestination versus free will, post-tribulation and pretribulation viewpoints, the baptism of the Holy Spirit and charismatic gifts. And often I would completely disagree with my parents. That's where the debates got fun, because I always felt so smart when little thirteen-year-old me could throw something into the conversation that could stump even my dad. (And when I did, he congratulated me!)

I knew full well that my parents struggled with many issues that are seen as core doctrines in the church. But rather than demanding my sister and I believe a certain way, seeing them wrestle with these complex topics gave us permission to work out our own salvation (Phil. 2:12). It wasn't weak to question what you believe. "These are arguments that people have been having for two thousand years, Rebecca," my dad would say, "Don't ever think that we've suddenly figured it all out now."

My parents taught us to think for ourselves because they modeled it and rewarded us when we did the same. And in doing so we learned that sincere Christians can believe differently on certain topics—and that it was okay.

WHY THE CHURCH ISN'T ENOUGH

No church is perfect. Humans run the church, and humans make mistakes. The Corinthian church allowed sexual sin in their congregation. The church in Galatia accepted false teachings. Peter, whom Christ appointed as the head of the church, refused to eat with Gentiles for a time because he was stuck in his old ways. Listen to what Paul says in Galatians about his confrontation with Peter:

> But when Peter came to Antioch, I had to oppose him to his face, for what he did was very wrong. When he first arrived, he ate with the Gentile believers, who were not circumcised. But afterward, when some friends of James came, Peter wouldn't eat with the Gentiles anymore. He was afraid of criticism from these people who insisted on the necessity of circumcision. As a result, other Jewish believers followed

Peter's hypocrisy, and even Barnabas was led astray by their hypocrisy. (2:11–13 NLT)

Then what does Paul do in the very next verse? He calls out Peter in front of everyone. Someone willing to hold a public confrontation doesn't strike me as someone who is concerned with saving face at all. Paul understood that just the fact that a person is wrong doesn't make him or her a horrible or unrighteous person. He also understood that if he didn't say something in front of those who had been led astray, they might never know the truth. And to Paul the truth always came first.

I think we have an idea that if you are wrong, you must be a bad person. The holy person is always right. Why don't we call out the pastor on something? Because we don't want to come across as holier-than-thou. I know this was a problem in my church; when I confronted my youth leader, he told me I was being judgmental and needed a lesson in humility. To him, being right was equated with being righteous.

When we unconsciously believe that being right is the same as being holy, we put pressure on the church to never admit it is wrong—because that would seem like admitting it is ungodly. We begin to defend it beyond any logical point rather than just dealing with the problem. When parents have the mentality that the church always needs to be supported because challenging it would be offensive, they begin to protect the church above all else—even truth. And that's when faith starts seeming fake to teenagers.

One year my youth group went on a huge youth retreat that had many other churches involved. I met my friend Josh there.

He was a freshman in high school, and it was his first big high school retreat.

One time, after a particularly moving service, Josh went outside for a walk to process everything he had just heard. He saw a girl from his youth group, who he knew struggled with cutting herself, crying on one of the docks. Immediately he went over to comfort her and pray with her. As they were praying for peace, a leader came up behind them and started yelling because they had broken the rule—they were of the opposite sex and alone together, even though they were on a dock in the daylight and in plain sight of the main building.

Later, in the dining hall, when everyone was together eating, the head leader of Josh's church came up to Josh and the girl and started yelling in front of everyone about how disrespectful to authority they had been for breaking the rules. I was embarrassed for them. The girl started crying, and Josh stood up and said, "This is ridiculous—we're supposed to be about Jesus, and I'm getting in trouble for praying with someone." The leaders wouldn't listen, though, and all of us in the dining room sat in awkward silence.

As soon as Josh's dad, who was acting as a chaperone for the guys, realized what was happening, he confronted the leaders, yelling back, "Don't shout at my kid! This is totally inappropriate." Later those leaders told Josh's father that unless he apologized for challenging authority, too, he would no longer be welcome as a youth leader or at any youth events. Just for standing up for his son, who had been trying to act like Jesus.

Since that incident, I have gone through the Plan to Protect program, which my church adheres to and which the youth retreat was under. The program mandates that all helpers, chaperones, and leaders complete a course to ensure the emotional, physical, and spiritual safety of all children involved in church activities. Public embarrassment and ridicule are definitely on the blacklist for that program, so Josh's dad was perfectly justified in speaking up. In fact, if that had happened in our church, we would have required the head leaders to step down from authority.

I really wish I could tell you that Josh's family continued to stand up for what was right, but I can't. After that threat, his father backed down and did apologize—even though no apology was ever given to Josh or that girl. Over the last five years, at different retreats, I have seen those same leaders yell at many other youths, and I've comforted quite a few girls left crying in the bathrooms.

I wish those church leaders and Josh's dad could have read Miller and Gur's study. Stressing obedience to church authority over authentic faith is an almost surefire recipe for kids to start leaving the faith entirely. Sometimes church leaders are wrong; Josh instinctively knew that at fourteen. His dad's first reaction was also that those leaders were wrong. But his dad allowed the leadership to make him submit, and in doing so, he showed his son that it was more important to obey authority, even if authority was wrong, than to act as Jesus did with the Samaritan woman.

IT'S ABOUT GOD, NOT THE CHURCH

Church is an amazing thing when God is leading it. But the church should be centered around God—not God around the church—and that's something that Lily's, Ethan's, and my parents all taught their children. It is something that Patrick learned after he had moved out, when he was finally able to ask questions and discover what it truly meant to live by the Spirit rather than by doing the right thing through his own willpower. And it is something Josh instinctively knew when he was fourteen but is now being told was wrong.

Allowing yourself to acknowledge that the church is not the fix-all to every problem and that it's okay to state truth (even if truth seems scary) allows you to also see the goodness of the church and God's community. You cannot appreciate the good until you know how to spot the bad. That was Patrick's problem, and that was my strength.

9

THE FAMILY AS A TEAM

EQUIPPING KIDS TO ANSWER GOD'S CALL

My parents met Betty and Sean Smith in university. As we grew up, they were always the cool family we went and visited every now and then. They had four kids—two girls Katie's and my ages and two boys who were older than us. It was a blast, because we could play house with the girls but also go tobogganing with the older boys (and they made the best tobogganing tracks).

They were, by all accounts, the perfect Christian family. The kids all got along, they would confide in their parents, and they were all heavily involved in their local church. The girls volunteered in children's ministry, and the boys volunteered with the worship team. It seemed idyllic.

But as they got older, Katie and I started to notice we had less and less in common with the kids. Sure, they were good kids. But they didn't seem to graduate from good kids to good adults. As

I went off to university, the oldest son—who was six years older than I was—was still living at home and didn't have any motivation to find a job. It was a failure-to-launch kind of situation. The second oldest was working toward a degree in business, but he was skating by and didn't seem to take anything seriously. The girls became increasingly obsessed with pop culture and cute guys, and although they stayed involved in church, it just never seemed to make a difference in their lives. They were culturally Christian, but it was hard to tell if it went further than skin-deep. Although they never rebelled, they definitely didn't thrive.

In writing this book, this family was at the back of my mind, gnawing away. They seemed like the perfect family—they checked off every box that I've talked about so far. But as their kids grew up, it became more difficult to talk to them about spiritual things. Their parents were frustrated that they weren't living up to the potential we all knew they had in droves. I really loved their parents—these were wonderful people. So what went wrong? Why are these kids not like the rest of us who didn't rebel, who are motivated to better our lives and have a deep, strong connection to our faith?

One of the things that united all the families who didn't rebel was that we had a sturdy sense of family identity. We identified strongly with our parents and siblings, we enjoyed being together, and we felt very much as if it was us against the world—in a good way. But this family would have said all those things too. And so I started thinking about different ways that we form family identity.

Families that enjoy each other and hang out together can

do so in one of two ways: they can be a club or they can be a team. In a club the main goal is to have fun. You're with a bunch of like-minded people, you hang out, you all enjoy each other's company, and you engage in activities you all enjoy. But it doesn't mean anything more than that.

A team, on the other hand, also has a strong sense of identity—but they have that identity because it's part of a bigger purpose. You're working toward something. While a club is about identity and having fun, a team has a goal. A team needs three things to function well: it needs to equip and train its players; it needs to develop a sense of cohesion, where all team members matter; and it needs a goal to work toward. That's quite different from a club, and I think it's the team mentality that was missing with our friends. Let's look at how each of these three things was lived out in families where kids didn't rebel.

TEAMS EQUIP THEIR PLAYERS

When Liam and I were six and seven, respectively, our favorite activity was starting fires. Literally. We went camping and our parents, wanting a few more hours of shut-eye, would let us go outside our tent trailers and play with the fire pit and see what we could burn. Our favorite things to burn were horse flies, since their bites hurt so much. (Looking back, our parents acknowledge it may have been a slightly inappropriate parenting decision.)

Remember Liam and Paul from chapter 4? Our family became close with their family when Liam and I were in kindergarten, and ever since then Liam and his little brother, Paul, and Katie and I have been like family. They helped at my wedding, Liam's mom and dad took me on my first four-wheeler ride, and Liam taught me how to play poker.

As I debated what potential differences there may have been between the Smiths' kids and the rest of us who didn't rebel, I thought of Liam. Not only did Liam not rebel—he thrived. Liam has a stellar track record—when he was sixteen he got his first official job working at a local factory. At eighteen he went off to college to become an electrician, while continuing to work on the side so he could graduate without student debt. Now, at only twenty, he has a full-time job, has bought his own car, and is about to move into his own apartment.

Moreover, Liam has maintained a strong faith. To me, Liam seems to be the flip side of the coin to the Smith children—he lived up to his potential, and he is thriving in the adult world. But how did this come about?

When talking to Liam, he believes the greatest contributing factor was that his family equipped him to grow up into a man. "Growing up, I was surrounded by the Wood legacy," Liam told me. "This legacy of good, hard, honest workers. There were so many stories about how hard my uncle Jack and my great-grandpa George worked on their farm. My parents are extremely hard workers. My dad and his brother, Dave, own a business together, and every day I see them wake up early in the morning, work hard all day, and come home beat but still have fun with their families. That's just what Woods do—we work hard, and we put family above all else."

Liam's dad, Derek, works a very physically demanding job, so often he'd come home exhausted. But Derek always ensured that family was a priority. "Even when my dad would come home really tired after a hard day of work, family time was nonnegotiable to him. So we always did something together, whether it was a hike in the woods or just a game of cards or a movie if Dad was too drained from the day. But no matter what, there was always family time. Even when we went away, my parents didn't just go away and leave the kids—vacation time was for the family and time was spent with the kids too." (A lot of that vacation time was spent camping with my family, which allowed for the parents to have some alone time by shipping all four of us kids to one campsite or the other.)

These family group events frequently allowed opportunities for Liam's dad to pass on wisdom to his teenage son. "Dad and I were cutting wood for the furnace one day, and we were just chatting while we worked when my dad said, 'When you grow up to be a man of a family, you need to work hard and provide for that family.' I was only around thirteen at the time, but it really got me to start thinking about what kind of a person I wanted to become."

Just passing down the stories of the Wood legacy isn't enough to equip someone to become an adult, though, and Liam's parents knew that. Liam's parents ensured that Liam and his brother, Paul, also learned by doing. "Everything we did was a team effort," Liam said. "If the hunting cabin's front porch needed to be repaired, we'd all go and fix it together, Mom included. We measured and cut the wood all together, and Dad would teach us on the job what we needed to do. But we were always expected to help out for as long as I can remember because we were family, and that's what family does."

After they had taught him how to be a hard worker, Liam's mom and dad encouraged him to look for opportunities to take on more adult responsibility. In grade ten, Liam got a job at a local factory, where he quickly excelled. His work ethic and dedication to the company made him stand out.

"The great part about working at the factory," Liam explained, "was that I got to save up so much money for college. I loved my job, and my parents were supportive of it. Here and there, my dad would say, 'I'm so proud of you for working hard, saving up for college, and making it easier for the family by making an effort to provide for your own schooling rather than putting the burden of your education on your parents. I'm very impressed with you.' It really solidified in my mind that working hard and being responsible with the money I made were the right things to do."

What I find so interesting about Liam's family was that even when he was a kid he was raised to become a good man. That doesn't mean he didn't have a fun childhood—we were complete goofballs, as are his parents. But what it does mean is that when he got older, taking on more and more responsibility wasn't scary. He was ready for it, and it didn't take him by surprise. Now Liam has successfully graduated from a two-year electrician degree, has a full-time job at the factory he worked at in high school, and is on the worship team at church. Liam's parents knew that it was not just about raising a good kid—it was about raising good kids who are ready to become good adults.

My family was all about equipping us to become adults too. I think this is one of the reasons we got along so well with the Woods—all of us kids were pretty much able to fend for ourselves. I was introduced to chores when I was three and could wipe off counters, even if I sometimes made more messes than I cleaned. By the time we were seven, Katie and I had each learned how to make eggs for breakfast and could easily make our own sandwiches for lunch. When I asked Mom if I could start babysitting for some spending money when I was twelve, she encouraged me to find some families at our church who were looking for someone to babysit once a week. At thirteen, my parents decided I was capable of monitoring my own schoolwork, and I was given pretty much full responsibility for ensuring that I got all my work done. When I started a business with one of my friends at fourteen, my mom lent us her credit-card reader so we could increase our sales.

My sister followed the same trajectory. My parents never shied away from giving us responsibility—they wanted us to become adults. Now, when I asked Mom about this, she replied, "Well, in reality I just wanted you to make your own breakfast sometimes because by the time you were seven, I was just sick and tired of doing it every morning. But I'm glad it taught you some responsibility."

Our parents, like Liam's, didn't treat us as though we were kids who needed to be taken care of; instead, they treated us like little adults. Liam's dad expected him to help with building the porch, and my parents expected us to be able to finish our schoolwork without them having to hover over our shoulder. It was always very clear to us that high school was just another stop on our way to adulthood, because our lives were oriented toward becoming responsible adults. My family had conversations around the dinner table about how much the food cost per serving, so Katie and I learned how to cook from scratch on a budget, starting when I was fourteen. I was saving for university from age three and continued to save up for the future through all my high school jobs.

As I talked about this with Liam, I realized that the emphasis on equipping kids to become self-sufficient was lacking in Betty and Sean's family. We first noticed this when Betty and Sean's girls were staying with us one March break while their parents were away and the boys were with a relative. Katie and I had a blast having the girls there, but they never seemed to be good at cleaning-up time. It was made clear from day one that since the girls were living here for a week, they would be expected to pitch in with family cleanup time, and they all agreed. But when it came down to actually doing the chores, that was another matter. The girls would sit at meals and wait to be served and would leave the table without clearing their dishes. But the straw that broke the camel's back for my mom was the night when it was Rachel's turn to do the dishes with me. Seeing me already starting to run the water while Rachel was reading a book, my mom reminded her, "Rachel, it's your turn to help with dishes."

Rachel promptly smiled and replied, "Oh, I can't do dishes. I have a skin condition."

My mom whipped out a pair of rubber gloves and said, "Lucky for you, I have some gloves that will keep your skin safe from the soap!"

The smile quickly disappeared, and Rachel did her first load of dishes that day. (My mom considers that one of her top-ten parenting moments.) Later, Rachel's mother explained that Rachel hadn't ever had to do chores, since she was still just a kid. At thirteen. I remember my mom being completely flabbergasted.

The thing about these kids is that they were fantastic kids. They grew into lovely teenagers who were a pleasure to be around. But as the years ticked by, they didn't seem to grow up. And I wonder if a lot of that is because they were never really equipped to become adults. When they turned eighteen and everyone else was excited for the future and had saved up thousands to go to school, they just stalled. They hadn't ever saved their money from the short-term jobs they had in high school, and they didn't really have any skills to help them integrate into the adult world, and as a result they just stayed in the high school mentality.

Unfortunately, that's where their faith stayed too. Their sons believe in God, but they don't make Him a part of their lives. Their youngest daughter has fallen away from the faith completely. It seems as though they were raised to be good Christian kids, but they just weren't equipped to become God-fearing adults.

FAMILY COHESION: TEAMS WORK TOGETHER

Equipping kids to be adults is important, but just because someone knows how to cook or how to build a deck doesn't mean that he or she will be ready *emotionally*. To emotionally be an adult, we must have the ability to think of others beyond ourselves and to know that the world does not revolve around us.

Unfortunately, many families unwittingly teach kids the exact opposite. Here's a scenario I witnessed time and time again while teaching swimming: often a mother would call multiple times throughout the week, trying frantically to sort out her son's swimming schedule so she could make her daughter's ballet recital without her son missing his half-hour splash class. She would try to move her son's lesson time to an hour earlier or an hour later, or even a completely different day, or she would warn me that someone else would be there to pick up little Jimmy (though she was still frantically trying to figure out who) because she just wasn't able to drive him to his swimming lessons at that time and couldn't find anyone else to drive him either. Sometimes it would even be because Mom had a doctor's appointment, and wasn't willing to let her child miss one swimming lesson so that she could get medical care.

I would stand there, dumbfounded, with my mouth open, trying to figure out how to respond. I was thinking, *Why don't you just take Jimmy to watch Jessie, so you can all clap wildly? Just skip the lesson!* But of course I didn't say that. I felt sorry for this mom, stressed-out while trying to make sure all the kids got to do what the kids wanted to do, without any sense of how to act like a family. Mom's goal was that no one would ever be inconvenienced, because she saw inconveniencing her kids as a personal failure rather than as a chance to teach her children how to sacrifice a bit of fun to support their team.

In families with kids who didn't rebel, the parents weren't

afraid to inconvenience their kids—it was just expected that everyone would drop what he or she was doing and show up to cheer each other on.

- "Whenever any of us had a show or a game or an award, the rest of us went. If my brother had a T-ball game, we all went to T-ball. If I was in a musical, they all came to my musical. It's always been that way, as long as I can remember— even after I moved out I came home to see my little brother graduate."
- "My brother and I were very different and were in different activities, but we always showed up for each other. Even though we didn't want to do the same things, we could still support each other in what we were interested in, so our parents made sure we did."
- "I was always expected to see all my sister's performances and competitions, and she came to all of mine. It didn't matter if we had anything else planned; we were just supposed to drop it and show up for each other."

But it wasn't only supporting siblings that was important. It was also about supporting the parents. Mom and Dad's health, well-being, and happiness matter too. And sometimes kids miss out on things because Mom and Dad have to make other choices, and that needs to be okay. In so many families, Mom has placed her entire identity into being a great mother. She sacrifices everything for them to make sure they have a great life. That's what Betty and Sean Smith did—Betty did all the housework and didn't demand anything of the kids, even to the point of exhausting herself. And the kids never learned to sacrifice for the greater good of the team.

In a team, all the members work together—one doesn't sacrifice for everyone else. There's true team cohesion where every member helps support everyone else. But in a lot of families, we don't see that cohesion. Instead, we see the parents catering to their children's every desire without expecting any sacrifice from their kids in return. Without learning to put aside our plans to support someone else, it's very easy to become self-centered and rely on others to take care of us. And that passivity doesn't lead to a child becoming equipped to be an adult.

My sister and I remember many times we missed music lessons or skating lessons because Mom was on a speaking tour and we didn't have anyone to drive us. But it couldn't be helped, and we were fine with that. When Mom was home, she always made sure that we never missed lessons (and never missed practicing either). Sometimes one family member misses out on something because of another family member's schedule. And that's okay, because that's what a family does.

FAMILY MISSION: TEAMS SHARE A COMMON GOAL

Jason, too, came from what looked like the perfect Christian family. Remember Ethan from chapter 8? His family had pretty much the same story. But unlike Ethan, Jason never made his faith his own.

Jason's parents were heavily involved in their church. They all pitched in, with his parents running the youth group and Jason on drums with the worship team. They went to all the youth rallies and never missed youth group. And Jason loved church during high school—he had friends there, there was free pizza at youth group, and he loved being in the worship band. But when he left for college, he simply stopped going to church. When his mom asked him why he hadn't gone to church his entire first semester at school, he just shrugged. "I don't know," he said. "I still believe in God. I just don't really think I need to go to church. What's the point?" He had walked out the church doors and never looked back.

As a millennial, I see this phenomenon play out over and over again with my generation, and I think it's because the focus of the modern church doesn't seem to mesh with millennials' values. Millennials' biggest value is justice. I saw a tweet once that said, "If we were in the middle of the zombie apocalypse I *swear* my generation would start a Zombie Rights campaign." And I think that's completely accurate. It's why many millennials are for gay marriage but are also against abortion, despite the two seeming to oppose each other. To millennials, it's a justice issue, not a moral one: everyone should have the right to love, and everyone should have the right to life.

On top of that, we live in the social media age, where with just a click you can see what's going on anywhere in the world. The world is more accessible now than it ever was before, and we who have grown up with that access are very aware that the world is so much more than just our neighborhoods—perhaps more aware than any generation has been before. The world has shrunk.

So when a family focuses all its attention on a church that's in their neighborhood and helps their community, it seems a bit shallow, to be honest. It's fun, and it's a lovely experience, but it seems irrelevant in this global age. It's as if you're paying yourself dues—you're volunteering somewhere that's going to help you in the long term, but doesn't seem to do anything for the world as a whole. Yes, many churches have a mission focus, and that should not be minimized. But often the mission focus includes giving to missionaries and having them speak once a year at the church to raise more funds. It can be hard to see how an individual church is making a real difference in the world. So for someone like Jason, as long as you're a good person, church doesn't really seem that important in the grand scheme of things.

Interestingly, many of the families who had kids who never thrived had thrown themselves into serving in the church, as had their children. But even that didn't seem to be enough for their kids to make their faith their own. From what I've found, families who had kids who didn't rebel tended to have a *kingdom* focus, not just a *church* focus. Their primary dedication was to furthering God's kingdom on earth, and they took it beyond the four walls of their churches.

This was always present in my family. I started tithing when I was three, when I started receiving an allowance for doing chores. Every Christmas, beginning when I was five or six, my aunt Allee would send us Harvest of Hope catalogs with a sum of money, and Katie and I got to choose how we were going to spend that money combined with our tithing money from the year. Usually we chose to give a family a goat or some chickens.

When I was eleven, we went on our first mission trip as a family to a children's home in Kenya called Mully Children's Family (MCF). The founder of MCF was formerly a street child himself, and he legally adopts every single child he rescues from the slums in Kenya. My nana had gone the year before, and we had been involved in fund-raising for this particular children's home for about a year when we went.

MCF changed my life. For the next five years I became heavily involved in organizing donations, visited Kenya two more times, and made friendships with the children over there that I still have today. Many of us are friends on Facebook and stay involved in each other's lives.

My parents wanted me to be exposed to Christianity across the world, and I'll tell you: singing about God's goodness with three hundred children who have all seen more suffering than I could imagine in a lifetime is humbling. And seeing how God had transformed their lives made me even more dedicated to making my faith my own. I wanted that transformation for myself.

After our 2006 and 2007 trips to Kenya, my parents wanted to go and live there for a year to work at a local hospital. They told Katie and me that this was something they felt strongly about and that it was a way they thought our family could really help spread God's love. They told us to pray about it and see if we felt called to it too.

Although we never ended up going, due to various signs from God (such as our acceptance letter showing up in the mail burned to a crisp), that was the mentality in our home. We, as a family, were put here to serve God. So the kids were also included in that calling. It was never Mom or Dad following God and us just tagging along—we were active participants in a greater calling, and we had a responsibility to work toward making this world a better one however we could.

As Katie and I grew older, we continued living out that mission focus. Katie started a YouTube channel so she could provide encouraging Christian entertainment. I started blogging to help challenge people to take their faith seriously. We found our own causes in adulthood because we were so used to working for something greater, it just seemed natural.

Many kids who didn't rebel had this greater focus throughout their childhood. Most had stories similar to Katie's and mine, where their families were heavily involved in overseas missions, or where they went on mission trips on their own in high school. Others did more community outreach, where their families were purposeful in inviting their non-Christian friends over and showing them love and acceptance. Some of them adopted children from overseas or became foster parents. Still others, like Joanna's family, chose a missions lifestyle.

Remember Joanna from chapter 5? Joanna's family attended a missions-focused church in the heart of Pittsburgh, but most of its members commuted in from the suburbs. "Our church was like an island in the inner city," explained Joanna, "and although they had many members from the suburbs, they couldn't seem to reach the people living downtown. One day, though, my parents went to a Christian conference and my dad felt called to move to the inner city to help breach that gap—not by acting as a missionary in the traditional sense, but simply by being a presence in the community.

"My dad felt very strongly about moving to the inner city," Joanna explained, "but my mom, although she knew Dad's calling was very real and for the whole family, hadn't felt it herself quite yet. So she prayed that God would reveal that calling to her too. As they started looking for houses, Mom wanted a historical home with a big yard, and for it to be a stand-alone property. That was hard to find in the inner city.

"After intense searching for a month, Mom couldn't find anything that fit her criteria and decided to surrender her list, since she knew that obeying God's call was more important than having her dream home. The very next Wednesday she found the house, and it was everything she wanted and more. By Thursday she had shown it to Dad and me; they signed the papers on Friday and sold our old house on Saturday for the exact amount they had bought the new one for." So when Joanna was two and her little brother was just a baby, they moved into an old historical house in the middle of the inner city.

Living in the inner city meant that Joanna's family lived in a culture that really wasn't theirs. "We didn't fit in," Joanna said. "It wasn't a good neighborhood. We'd have the odd belligerent man screaming at people on the street, and I wasn't allowed to walk the dog without carrying Mace with me. There was even a porn theater down the street from our house. It had all these bright lights, so growing up my brother and I would get excited and say, 'Mommy! It's a circus! Can we go there?'

"My mom, holding back her laughter, would just tell us, 'No, sweetie.'

"'Why not?' we'd ask.

"'Well, honey,' she'd explained, 'that's a place people go to sin.'"

Joanna laughed. "Yeah, we were definitely not part of the culture of our neighborhood."

Joanna's parents wanted to include their children in this missions-based lifestyle. One of the ways they did that was through the school they chose. Her parents wanted their children to go to a school that was strong academically but was also in the city. This school helped the inner city become the children's normal and gave them the opportunity to be included in ministry. As well, Joanna's parents were purposeful in talking with their children about their calling.

"We kids truly felt that God had called us to the inner city," said Joanna, "and our family was really fun, so we didn't mind standing out. I grew up with the stories about how God had provided our house, and my parents openly talked to us about the importance of ministering in diverse communities, and they often reminded us that diversity included socioeconomic diversity too."

This open communication about the family's ministry kindled a passion in Joanna for spreading God's love. Joanna smiled as she told me. "When I was in first grade, I was an extremely zealous child, and I would chat with a friend of mine from church on the bus going to school. We decided one day that we were going to make a Save the Whales club, because they needed saving. Then we thought, *But wait . . . we need a Save the People club so we can bring them to the Lord!"* Joanna laughed. "We were so excited about it, but it didn't work so well. But, ironically, we also started a Batman club where we actually *did* lead a lot of kids to Christ, even though that wasn't the aim at all.

"Having a missions focus growing up shaped who I am and definitely helped me and my siblings not to rebel," Joanna said. "I always felt that when I was older, I'd be a missionary and I'd do big things for God when I had grown up. But growing up I realized that I already felt like I was a part of it, even though I was just a kid. I think a lot of it is because we went to the school that we did—we had that mission to reach diverse groups of people, not just people who were the same as us, and our school gave us opportunities to live out that mission ourselves. The call was so inclusive that it didn't stop at where we lived or where we went to school. It just became our approach to life—helping people meet Jesus wherever they were."

Joanna's family challenged their children to make their faith their own by allowing them to do real work for God, even as children. Getting involved in something greater than your-self sometimes requires getting involved in something greater than your church. Jason's problem was that church didn't seem to change anything—it was just another club he was a part of. But for Joanna's family and mine, Christianity had a much wider reach. We were in a position to see God really move in the lives of people around us. To us, going to church meant becoming equipped for the calling that God had for us outside the church walls, and that was much too important for us to give up.

EQUIPPING KIDS TO ANSWER THE CALL

Looking at all these stories, it's clear that the main difference between families who had children who did rebel and families who had children who didn't comes to this: families with children who did rebel acted like a club; families with children who didn't rebel acted like a team.

A team has a goal. The players are trained intensely to be able to achieve that goal, and they're expected to take responsibility for their own training too. They are expected to grow, to become more and more skilled, so that someday they'll be ready for the big game. It's the same with team-oriented families. Families whose kids truly thrived and stayed strong in their faith had a goal: to follow God's calling as a family and to equip their children to follow His calling for their own lives. From early on these kids were involved in serving God beyond their church's four walls—they saw Him in action, they saw Him making a real difference. These kids were trained to become not only good kids, but to grow up into God-fearing adults. They were just as fun as the other families, but it went further—it was about more than just being nice. It was about making a difference. So when they became adults and had to take on real responsibility for the first time, they were ready for it.

Raising kids who don't rebel is more than just raising good kids. It's about equipping kids to go on themselves to bravely follow God's calling. As James 1:27 says: "Religion that God our Father accepts as pure and faultless is this: to look after orphans and widows in their distress and to keep oneself from being polluted by the world."

So let's be a team that's focused on bringing God's kingdom to earth. That's so much bigger, and more meaningful, than just having fun.

10

WORKS IN PROGRESS

BEFORE THE PRODIGAL RETURNS

I've focused in this book on giving some ideas and encouragement about how to raise kids who are less likely to rebel. But I know many families are walking through rebellion right now. Many of you reading this are in the middle of a dark time as a parent—your teen is getting involved in partying, drugs, drinking, sex, or is just generally not following God's desire for him or her.

So I wanted to offer some encouragement by sharing stories from some of the people I interviewed who were once in the same place, but who aren't anymore, to show that rebellion is not necessarily the end of your story.

WHEN YOU DO EVERYTHING RIGHT, BUT IT ALL STILL GOES WRONG

KAYLA'S STORY

Kayla's parents divorced when she was two, due to her mother needing to leave an unhealthy relationship. Both of her parents remarried by the time she was five. Growing up, Kayla would spend weekends with her dad and stepmom and live with her mom and stepdad during the week.

"My dad's place seemed to be the best place on earth—I wasn't ever punished, but I'd get disciplined at my mom's house, so as a kid I thought my dad was the coolest. Growing up, my stepmom and dad would tell me, 'This is your home too. You're our daughter. You should live here.' I felt so loved and wanted to be with them. When I was twelve my dad and stepmom had a baby girl, and two years later they had a little boy. But they still said they wanted me to live with them too."

Everything changed one night when Kayla had just started high school. "I had forgotten my retainer at my dad's house, so I needed to go and get it. I knocked a couple of times and could see my little sister watching me from the window. So I walked into the house, since I had been told it was my home, and saw my stepmom at the top of the stairs. She started yelling at me, 'This isn't your home! You shouldn't be here! Get out!'"

I saw Kayla wince as she told the story.

"I went to find my dad at his work, crying, and explained that his wife wasn't letting me in the house. But he just made excuses and didn't even let me grab my retainer. I haven't spent any real time with them since."

You can imagine that high school didn't go so well after the incident. "I did rebel in high school," Kayla told me. "I was living with my mom and stepdad full-time, and I just stopped caring. I didn't do schoolwork, and I lied about everything. My dad and stepmom had taught me how to lie from a young age, telling me things like, 'Don't tell your mom and stepdad about anything that happens here.' They really trained me to become a liar."

Kayla's relationship with her mom and stepdad was, frankly, horrible. They fought constantly, and Kayla's mom watched in agony as her daughter seemed to give up. "I was dishonest about everything I could possibly lie about," Kayla explained, "even things I didn't have to. And it really took a toll on my mom. At one point it got so bad that I actually had to go stay with our youth pastor's family for a night so my mom and I could have some space." The lying and the broken relationship was putting a huge strain on both Kayla and her mother and made the relationship extremely difficult.

"I knew they loved me," Kayla explained, "and I knew they wanted the best for me, but I kept acting out because I didn't feel that I deserved the best because of how my dad and step-mom treated me." Kayla shrugged. "I didn't feel like I was good enough."

Kayla's mom and stepdad, however, never gave up on her. They were both Christians and made church a priority for Kayla. She was encouraged to become part of a Christian traveling arts group and became heavily involved in a youth group during her teenage years, where she made friendships she's kept to this day.

"My parents were strict with me, and I think it's because they saw that I really needed that structure to help me get my life back together after it had fallen apart so abruptly. So church became a natural part of my life, and one of the biggest parts of my life socially. But I was still hurting, and that affected my relationship with my mom and stepdad."

Kayla had been antsy to leave home and just be on her own since she was fourteen, so as soon as she graduated high school, she moved from Ontario to Alberta to go to school. And she hated it. "It was awful," Kayla said. "I was at a Christian school, but I felt like my relationship with God was being judged and I didn't know where I fit in. On top of all that, my grandfather passed away, and I wasn't even able to make the funeral because I was stuck at school all the way out in Alberta. It was a terrible time. To top it off, after I got my EMR license, I only just barely failed my EMT license exam. I was devastated."

Kayla found a job in a flower shop, but that didn't turn out any better. "I had the worst boss in the world," Kayla said with a laugh. "It was truly horrendous. But that was the breaking point for me. While I was in Alberta, going through all this," Kayla explained, "everything piled up and made me realize that I needed to make changes in my life."

As she was out in Alberta, alone, reaching rock bottom, she thought about her mom and stepdad and about how they had always been there for her. "I started realizing that my parents had always truly loved me—something I had never believed before because of what happened with my dad. I just hadn't understood because I was a kid traveling between two completely different homes. But I looked back and saw how concerned my mom and stepdad had always been for me, their continued support, and how they never left me even after everything I had put them through in high school."

Kayla started realizing that a lot of the issues with her relationship with her mom were not because of her mom, but because of her relationship with her dad. "I hadn't felt that my parents truly understood me," Kayla explained, "but I realized that although I never actually talked to my parents about what was going on, I knew that I could."

Kayla smiled and said, "I think I just needed to get to such a bad place that I was finally willing to let God in and hear Him say to me, 'No, they aren't lying—they really love you.'"

Kayla moved back to her hometown, where she joined her parents' family business. Her relationship with her mom and stepdad is fantastic now. After more than twenty years of having her stepdad raise her, she decided to go through the adoption process and have him legally adopt her. She also took his last name. Her mom and stepdad were thrilled—and so was Kayla.

When I asked Kayla what her parents could have done differently, she told me that she didn't think they did anything wrong. "Mom and Dad did everything they could," Kayla explained. "They did everything right—I just needed to find healing before I'd be okay."

Even when you do everything right, sometimes God has to reach your child first. Kayla had hurts that didn't allow her to have a strong relationship with her mom and stepdad, but they created the structure and opportunities for her to learn about God. And then God reached her when she was thousands of miles away from home.

WHEN YOU DON'T PARENT PERFECTLY, BUT GOD DOES

But what if you *have* done things wrong and that's one of the reasons why your child rebelled? It definitely doesn't mean that your child's story is over.

PATRICK'S STORY

Patrick came from a family that, although they said all the right things, seemed to lack the genuine love and grace of Christ in their home.

"Although I knew my parents were Christian," Patrick explained, "and I was raised as a Christian, it never seemed authentic. It didn't seem to matter. So although I knew that sin was wrong, it seemed a lot of the time like it was an uphill battle I could never win." Patrick's face fell. "I didn't want to fall away, but I had so many religious goals for myself that I felt I needed to reach, and I was constantly failing them. I felt like I just couldn't do it, and I was constantly in a spiritual battle by myself. I was so tired."

When he got to university, he gave up. "I figured that I was an adult, and I could do whatever I wanted. So I did. That's when I got really involved in partying, sex, dabbling in drugs, and vandalism." Patrick shrugged. "But by the end of the first semester, I realized this wasn't fulfilling me either. And I knew I needed to make a change."

Patrick's roommates were strong, authentic Christians. For the first time he found believers who seemed to have a faith that really transformed their lives. And through getting involved in a Spirit-filled Christian community, Patrick finally found the relationship with Jesus that he had been yearning for throughout high school. Rather than simply accepting another rules-based religion, he had found the Spirit.

Even though it wasn't perfect from then on, the battle was very different for Patrick. Now he wasn't fighting alone, because he was in a real relationship with God rather than trying to check off boxes and win God's favor. Since then, Patrick has made a complete turnaround. He went from struggling with sexual sin to being part of the Fight the New Drug campaign.

"I'm still working through things," Patrick admits, "but ever since I made that choice, it's been a steady improvement. I have setbacks, but I know that living for God is the only place to find what I was missing from life."

NATHAN'S STORY

Nathan, if you recall from chapter 2, was raised in a very rules-based environment. When he moved cities in his final year of high school, he found himself in with a new peer group that was much more involved in partying than his friends from his hometown.

"During my rebellion stage," Nathan explained, "I was mad because we had moved, and I'd left all my friends and my girlfriend back at my old town. As well, my mom was still trying to push all these rules on me that didn't make any sense, even though I was only going to be living at home for another year. So I was so angry and frustrated with losing my friends, as well as having to deal with all these illogical rules, that I just started blatantly disregarding them.

"I was dating my girlfriend from back home, Tracy, for the majority of my rebellion stage," Nathan said, "and she definitely egged me on. It was a bad match, and we really brought out the worst in each other. And my parents didn't like the relationship either, which made me want to keep it going even more. It was a really rough time."

After a year, though, Nathan came to a new understanding. "Just before I graduated high school, I broke up with Tracy after realizing she was flirting with other guys when I wasn't there. It was really hard for me, but it knocked some sense into me. I realized how incredibly immature we had been, over the last year in particular, and how shallow she was. And I noticed that through getting into the party scene and dating her, I was becoming a very immature, shallow person. And I knew I didn't want that.

"I started getting serious about my life," Nathan explained. "I went to college, got my first real job, and I started looking for a girl who would challenge me to be a better person. Most of all, though, I realized that I wanted to be the kind of man my dad is, and to do that I needed to get right with God."

Realizing this prompted Nathan to make real changes in his life. Now he is married to an amazing woman from a great Christian family who isn't afraid to challenge him to continue his growth, especially in his faith.

I know that many of you who are reading this book may be thinking, *I wish I had raised my children differently*. But know that it's not too late—it wasn't for Patrick, it wasn't for Nathan, and it isn't for your child either, because God can still do His work.

WHEN YOU'RE UNABLE TO PARENT WELL, AND THE BODY OF CHRIST STEPS IN

LILA'S STORY

What about if you're not in a place where you're able to do everything right? What if you're going through heartbreak, or something really hard, and you just don't know how you're going to be there for your kids in the way you want to?

Remember Lila from chapter 4? When her parents divorced, her mom just wasn't able to talk to her about it because she hadn't dealt with it herself. So their relationship suffered. And her dad wasn't much help in the emotions department either. "He didn't really get how to talk about feelings and emotions," Lila explained, "so we talked mainly about other things, like school, politics, and global issues. Not what I was going through."

For Lila, however, her parents' inability to be there for her emotionally didn't mean she was left alone. "I was so lucky to find an amazing church," Lila said. "When my mom started to go to a church a couple blocks away from home, it had a youth group program, and the pastor invited me to a girl's small group. I wasn't too thrilled about it at first, but I started going, and it changed everything for me."

Lila smiled while she described her small group. "I could go, pour out my heart, and people would truly listen and then point me toward God. It was that group that caused me to start taking my faith seriously, and I decided to follow Jesus."

Today Lila is involved with the IVCF group on her campus and doing better than ever. Her relationship with her parents has improved as well, both because more time has passed since the divorce and also because living far away makes it easier to communicate without anyone feeling attacked or defensive.

"Now that I'm an adult and far away from home, I've really grown because of my faith, when I talk to them, they don't feel as directly impacted. Now it's easier for them to see what I'm going through as my problem, not just my problem with something they did. It's helped our relationship a lot. But without my church I don't know if I would have gotten there."

SONIA'S STORY

Sometimes, though, parents aren't able to help their child, not because they are emotionally unavailable, but because they're not physically available.

Sonia didn't run into trouble until after she had left home. Growing up she was a gracious, thoughtful, deliberate Christian girl. She had goals for her life, she didn't give in to peer pressure, and she had a very firm concept of who she was.

That all changed one night when she was sexually assaulted, two months after leaving home to study at university four hours away.

Though her parents did their best to try to get Sonia

counseling and help her through this time, she pulled away. Unable to process what had happened, Sonia made some bad choices over the next few years and fell into terrible relationships. "I got into one relationship in particular that was very bad," Sonia explained. "I had been so hurt, and I just wanted to feel happy again. He liked me, and we started going out. Soon we were sleeping together, and even though he was manipulative and mean, I stuck with him."

While all this was going on, her parents could do nothing but be a listening ear and pray—a ton. But then, two years later, it all changed for Sonia.

"I didn't realize how much it was hurting me until I hit rock bottom. I found out that the guy I was dating was sleeping with other girls, and at this point I had spent thousands on him, helping him with rent and car payments and the like. But I was done—especially when I realized he had a kid with some other girl. So I left him, and I was back to square one, with hardly any money in the bank and just as heartbroken as ever."

When Sonia left her boyfriend, she couldn't afford to live on her own anymore, so she moved back in with her parents. Living with them, she started to think back on who she had been as a teen and how much happier she had been before all these horrible things happened.

"I decided that it was enough," Sonia said. "I was so tired of feeling hurt. Finally, I turned to God and let Him start to heal me of the horrible things I had gone through. And I'm so glad I did."

Today Sonia is a confident young woman again, making new plans for her future and about to embark on a career in the military. Those wandering years were terrible for her parents, but the foundation her parents had created for her throughout her childhood—teaching her truths about God and His redeeming love—is what helped bring her to healing when she was ready.

Sometimes parents just aren't able to parent well because there is something in the way. Courtney's mom was overwhelmed with her own depression and her son's behavioral issues. Lila's mom was overwhelmed with grief and guilt from the divorce. Sonia's parents were powerless because of physical distance. Parents are not always able to do what is best for their children. But maybe that's why God put us in a body of believers—so that the body can step in when we can't. God doesn't leave you in the lurch. As Matthew 10:29–31 says:

> Are not two sparrows sold for a penny? Yet not one of them will fall to the ground outside your Father's care. And even the very hairs of your head are all numbered. So don't be afraid; you are worth more than many sparrows.

FINAL WORDS

Throughout this book we've looked at a lot of different ways that families helped their kids not rebel. But it all boils down to one thing: authenticity. That's what called Kayla back to her family, that's what Lila found in her youth group, and that's what Patrick was longing for. Authenticity is what allows parents to have a relationship with their children in a way that openly and honestly shows how God has been working in their lives. All the other things, like our preconceived notions of what a good Christian family should look like, get in the way.

- Instead of rules that help dictate behavior to create "perfect" children, we need parents who will train us to make our own decisions, even if that can be messy at times.
- Instead of being told we're the best, we need to learn that our identity is in Christ alone, even if we come in last place.
- Instead of being expected to fail, we want to know that you believe in our ability to succeed.
- Instead of using discipline to stifle bad behavior, teach us why we should choose good behaviors, so that by the time we're teens, discipline isn't an issue.
- Instead of talking to us only to get the inside scoop, communicate with us simply because you truly want to know us as people.
- Instead of simply being a family by blood, we need somewhere to belong so that when we're missing out on the parties we know we have something better.
- Instead of simply going to church, we need to see true faith.

And finally, instead of simply being raised to be good kids, we need to be equipped to be God-fearing adults, ready to further His kingdom.

I hope you've been encouraged after reading this book. I don't want to be just another voice telling you, "You can't do it. It's impossible." Because, as I hope you now know, that statement is so incredibly false. I hope that the stories in this book have shown you that there *is* hope, and that raising kids who don't rebel boils down to simply getting to know your kids and letting them get to know you too—even if you make mistakes along the way.

I am eternally grateful that my parents took the time and the effort not just to parent us but to truly coach us into becoming adults who were equipped to serve God's kingdom in big ways. Even though they weren't perfect, their encouragement and support have been the most consistent reflection of God's love that I could have asked for as a child.

Forget all the gimmicks; just get back to the basics of getting to know your kids. Then kids are far less likely to rebel, because they have everything they need: they have you. And whether you fully feel it or not, God created you for this. You love your kids. Live out that love naturally, and see your kids blossom into men and women who run to God with all their hearts.

ACKNOWLEDGMENTS

I think the first person I need to thank is my stats professor. If you hadn't delivered one of the most boring lectures I have ever experienced, I may never have written the blog post that turned into this book. I also owe thanks to everyone who read and shared that initial blog post. You had no idea that with a simple click of a button, you were pushing me toward a dream I never even knew I had. I even thank those couple of haters I had. Because you know what? You helped drive that view count up. Bet that didn't go how you expected.

A huge thank-you to my agent, Chip, who has truly gone above and beyond to help me find my footing as a new author. Plus, he's a pretty great Nashville tour guide to boot. To my editor, Webster, who somehow managed to make me enjoy having my work edited (I am a perfectionist with a stubborn, prideful streak—that was quite a feat).

To the amazing men and women whom I interviewed for this book. You all blew me away with your graciousness and deep insights into your teenage years. Thank you for allowing me to tell your stories, and I hope I did them justice.

Of course, I also need to thank my wonderful husband. Connor, I could not have done this without you. Thank you for being my voice of reason through this process, and for reminding me that, no, pizza and Starbucks should not be diet staples, and I should still eat broccoli, even when I have an entire book to write. You have taken such good care of me, and I am so glad that I could go on this adventure with you.

To my grandparents Ron, Cheryl, and Elizabeth. Grandma and Grandpa, how much you two have believed in me has shaped who I am today. I may have taken my husband's name, but I'll always be proud to call myself a Gregoire. Nana, thank you for all the years of prayer that I know you have poured into my life. You are one of the wisest people I know, and watching your example of faith has infinitely strengthened my own.

To my mom, who has always supported me, always loved me, and always called me her special snowflake. Oh no, wait— that's someone else's mom.

To *my* mom (Sheila at tolovehonorandvacuum.com), who drove three hours just to sit beside me on the couch and force me to write the book proposal, telling me to "suck it up. This is a good idea; you'll regret it if you don't." It turns out you were right.

Daddy, thank you for the entire last two years, as I was pitching and writing this book. You've always been my rock when I feel so stressed I might explode. All those hour-long phone calls where you encouraged me and prayed over me will be cherished forever.

And last, and perhaps most important, I want to say thank you to my baby sister, Katie (youtube.com/katiegregoire). We've come a long way, from you drawing me with devil horns and my LITTLE SISTERS KEEP OUT signs for my bedroom door. Thank you for listening to me talk about the same problem again and again until I finally found the answer. You are my best friend, and I could never have taken on a project like this without you in my life.

ABOUT THE AUTHOR

REBECCA GREGOIRE LINDENBACH is a writer and blogger who lives with her husband, Connor, in Ottawa, Canada. She is an online entrepreneur passionate about challenging common Christian patterns of thought, and hopes someday to be the proud owner of a mangy rescue mutt. For information about Rebecca speaking at your parenting event or with her mother at your mother-daughter event, contact her through lifeasadare.com.

NOTES

CHAPTER 1: WHAT IS REBELLION?

1. Erik H. Erikson, "Reflections on the Dissent of Contemporary Youth," *International Journal of Psychoanalysis* 51, no. 1 (1970): 12.

CHAPTER 2: RULES VERSUS REASONS

1. Keisha M. Love and Deneia M. Thomas, "Parenting Styles and Adjustment Outcomes Among College Students," *Journal of College Student Development* 55, no. 2 (2014): 140, doi:10.1353/csd.2014.0013.

2. Ibid.

3. Ibid.

4. Ibid., 139.

5. Paloma Braza et al., "Negative Maternal and Paternal Parenting Styles as Predictors of Children's Behavioral Problems: Moderating Effects of the Child's Sex," *Journal of Child and Family Studies* 24, no. 4 (2015): 847–56, doi:10.1007/s10826-013-9893-0; Ann Thompson, Chris Hollis, and David Richards, "Authoritarian Parenting Attitudes as a Risk for Conduct Problems," *European Child and Adolescent Psychiatry* 12, no. 2 (2003): 84–91, doi:10.1007/s00787-003-0324-4.

CHAPTER 3: EXPECTATIONS

1. Dennis V. Ary et al., "The Influence of Parent, Sibling, and Peer Modeling and Attitudes on Adolescent Use of Alcohol," *International Journal of the Addictions* 28, no. 9 (1993): 872, doi:10.3109/10826089309039661.

2. Susan G. Nash, Amy McQueen, and James H. Bray, "Pathways to Adolescent Alcohol Use: Family Environment, Peer Influence, and Parental Expectations," *Journal of Adolescent Health* 37, no. 1 (2005): 27, doi: 10.1016/j.jadohealth.2004.06.004.

3. Stephen B. Graves and Elizabeth Larkin, "Lessons from Erikson: A Look at Autonomy Across the Lifespan," *Journal of Intergenerational Relationships* 4, no. 2 (2006): 63–64, doi: 10.1300/J194v04n02UL05.

4. Ibid., 65.

5. Ibid.

CHAPTER 4: COMMUNICATION

1. World Health Organization, "Mental Disorders Affect One in Four People: Treatment Available but Not Being Used," WHO, October 4, 2001, http://www.who.int/whr/2001/media_centre /press_release/en/.

2. Cindy H. Liu et al., "U.S. Caregivers with Mental Health Problems: Parenting Experiences and Children's Functioning," *Psychiatric Nursing* 30, no. 6 (2016): 753–60, doi:dx.doi.org/10.1016 /j.apnu.2016.07.006.

3. Ibid.

4. Alicia Borre and Wendy Kliewer, "Parental Strain, Mental Health Problems, and Parenting Practices: A Longitudinal Study," *Personality and Individual Differences* 68, no. 1 (2014): 96, doi:10.1016/j.paid.2014.04.014.

5. Sylia Wilson and C. Emily Durbin, "Effects of Paternal Depression on Fathers' Parenting Behaviors: A Meta-Analytic Review," *Clinical Psychology Review* 30, no. 2 (2010): 177,

doi:10.1016/j.cpr.2009.10.007; Cynthia Ewell Foster, Judy Garber, and Joseph Durlak, "Current and Past Maternal Depression, Maternal Interaction Behaviors, and Children's Externalizing and Internalizing Symptoms," *Journal of Abnormal Child Psychology* 36, no. 4 (2008): 534, doi:10.1007/s10802-007-9197-1.

CHAPTER 5: FRIENDSHIP

1. Shira Offer, "Family Time Activities and Adolescents' Emotional Well-Being," *Journal of Marriage and Family* 75, no. 1 (2013): 37, doi: 10.1111/j.1741-3737.2012.01025.x.
2. Ibid.
3. Ibid., 38.

CHAPTER 6: DISCIPLINE

1. Elizabeth T. Gershoff and Andrew Grogan-Kaylor, "Spanking and Child Outcomes: Old Controversies and New Meta-Analyses," *Journal of Family Psychology* 30, no. 4 (2016): 454, doi:10.1037/fam0000191.
2. Elisa Romano, PhD, in discussion with the author, July 2016.
3. Samuel Martin, *Thy Rod and Thy Staff They Comfort Me: Christians and the Spanking Controversy* (Jerusalem: Sorensic: 2006), 32.
4. Romano, discussion with author.

CHAPTER 7: REALITY-BASED PARENTING

1. Roy F. Baumeister et al., "Does High Self-Esteem Cause Better Performance, Interpersonal Success, Happiness, or Healthier Lifestyles?" *Psychological Science* 14, no. 1 (2003): 1–44.
2. Claudia Mueller and Carol Dweck, "Praise for Intelligence Can Undermine Children's Motivation and Performance," *Journal of Personality and Social Psychology* 75, no. 1 (1998): 33–52, doi:10.1037/0022-3514.75.1.33.
3. Ibid., 36.
4. Ibid., 37.

5. Angela Duckworth and James J. Gross, "Self-Control and Grit: Related but Separable Determinants of Success," *Current Directions in Psychological Science* 23, no. 5 (2014): 320, doi:10.1177/0963721414541462.

6. Ibid.

CHAPTER 8: IT'S ABOUT GOD, NOT THE CHURCH

1. R. E. Dew et al., "A Prospective Study of Religion/Spirituality and Depressive Symptoms Among Adolescent Psychiatric Patients," *Journal of Affective Disorders* 120, no. 1 (2010): 154–55; Robert D. Laird, Loren D. Marks, and Matthew D. Marrero, "Religiosity, Self-Control, and Antisocial Behavior: Religiosity as a Promotive and Protective Factor," *Journal of Applied Developmental Psychology* 32, no. 2 (2011): 79, 83, doi: 10.1016/j.appdev.2010 .12.003; Kyle C. Longest and Stephen Vaisey, "Control or Conviction: Religion and Adolescent Initiation of Marijuana Use," *Journal of Drug Issues* 38, no. 3 (2008): 707, http://www .stephenvaisey.com/documents/controlorconviction.pdf.

2. Lisa Miller and Merav Gur, "Religiousness and Sexual Responsibility in Adolescent Girls," *Journal of Adolescent Health* 31, no. 5 (2002): 403–5, doi:10.1016/S1054-139X(02)00403-2.

3. Ibid., 403.

4. Ibid.

5. Longest and Vaisey, "Control or Conviction," 707.